Impressum

Band 5 der Reihe „Schau, so geht das!“
Velber Verlag

Illustrationen: Detlef Kersten
Coverfoto: Christoph Schmotz
Experimente-Fotos: Christoph Schmotz (9, 11, 13, 15, 17, 19, 21, 23, 25, 27, 29, 31, 33, 35, 37, 39, 41, 43, 45)
sonstige Fotos: arco (22, 38); dpa (10, 12, 16, 18, 20, 34, 36, 42); Katja Foggin (40); NASA (30); Ulrich Niehoff (14); NOVA (26); Michael Rhode (8, 28); Reinhard Wilde (24)

Text und Redaktion: Ulrike Berger
Layout: Anja Schmidt
Repro: Otterbach Medien GmbH & Co. KG, Rastatt
Druck und Bindung: Nørhaven Book A/S, Viborg

velber

Die Kräfte-Werkstatt

Spannende Experimente mit Kraft und Gleichgewicht

Inhalt

Die Wunder der Welt

Viele spannende Experimente zum Thema Schwerkraft, Fliehkraft und Gleichgewicht warten in diesem Buch auf euch. Was ihr dafür braucht, gibt es in fast jedem Haushalt.
Manche Experimente könnt ihr alleine durchführen, andere gehen leichter, wenn euch jemand hilft.
Und falls ein Experiment nicht sofort gelingt: Nicht den Mut verlieren! Einfach probieren, bis es klappt. Forscher brauchen Geduld. Doch es lohnt sich, denn bei jedem Experiment werdet ihr ein wenig mehr von den großen Wundern dieser Welt verstehen!

Das mutige Pendel

Du brauchst:
- einen Ball an einer Schnur

Befestige die Schnur (zum Beispiel mit einem Nagel) an der Decke oder dem Türrahmen, sodass der Ball frei schwingen kann. Ziehe ihn zu dir. Wenn möglich, lehne deinen Kopf an die Wand. Dann hältst du den Ball genau an deine Nase und lässt ihn los – bewege dich nicht, es kann dir nichts passieren!

Was passiert?
Der Ball kommt zwar wieder zurück – da er aber durch die Luft etwas abgebremst wird, wird er nie mehr bis zu deiner Nase zurückkehren. Daran ist der „Luftwiderstand" schuld.

Radeln gegen den Wind

Radfahren kann ganz schön anstrengend sein. Vor allem, wenn ein heftiger Gegenwind weht. Da kommt man manchmal kaum vom Fleck! Aber auch sonst gilt: Die meiste Kraft (mehr als die Hälfte!) beim Radeln brauchst du, um den Luftwiderstand zu überwinden.

Eine faule Münze

Du brauchst:

- ein Glas
- eine Spielkarte
- eine Münze

Lege die Karte mit der Münze auf das Glas. Wetten, du kannst die Münze ins Glas fallen lassen, ohne die Münze zu berühren? Du musst nur kräftig gegen die Karte schnippen oder sie mit einem kurzen Ruck wegziehen.

Was passiert?

Wenn du die Karte wegschnippst oder mit einem kurzen Ruck wegziehst, bewegt sich die Münze nicht mit. Denn die Münze ist faul – man spricht hier von „Trägheit“. Sie braucht ein bisschen, um sich in Bewegung zu setzen. Doch dann ist es bereits zu spät: Die Karte ist weg – und die Münze fällt ins Glas!

Unbedingt festhalten!

Alle Körper sind faul – das hat der Wissenschaftler Isaac Newton herausgefunden. Deswegen kippt man auch so leicht nach hinten, wenn der Bus anfährt und man sich nicht festgehalten hat!

50 EURO CENT

Kraft durch Wasser

Du brauchst:
- einen Plastikschlauch
- zwei Ballons (Wasserbomben)
- zwei Plastikflaschen
- zwei Gläser

Bohre in beide Flaschen unten ein Loch und schneide den Flaschenhals ab. Stecke einen Ballon auf den Schlauch und fülle den Schlauch und den Ballon mit Wasser. Dann legst du den Ballon in eine Flasche, führst den Schlauch durch das Loch hinaus und in die andere Flasche hinein. Fülle auch den zweiten Ballon mit Wasser und stülpe ihn über das andere Ende des Schlauchs. Setze beide Gläser auf die Ballons. Drücke nun auf ein Glas.

Was passiert?
Das Wasser schiebt sich durch den Schlauch in den anderen Ballon hinein – und das andere Glas wird nach oben geschoben.

Hydraulik

Bagger arbeiten mit solchen „hydraulischen" Kräften – nur nicht mit Wasser, sondern mit anderen Flüssigkeiten. An einer Stelle wird durch eine Art Spritze Druck auf die Flüssigkeit ausgeübt. Diese wird durch die Stangen zur Schaufel gepumpt und kann dort große Lasten bewegen!

Der berühmte Eiertest

Du brauchst:
- ein rohes Ei
- ein gekochtes Ei

Wie kannst du herausfinden, welches Ei roh und welches gekocht ist? Lege beide Eier auf den Tisch und drehe sie gleichzeitig ganz leicht.

Was passiert?
Das gekochte Ei dreht sich sofort. Das rohe Ei jedoch braucht etwas Zeit, um sich in Bewegung zu setzen. Denn das flüssige Eiweiß ist träge und will sich zuerst nicht mitdrehen. Das Ei taumelt, es wackelt und hört auch bald wieder mit dem Drehen auf.

Warum wird uns schwindelig?

Dein Gleichgewichtssinn ist im Innenohr. Dort sind ringförmige Schläuche, die mit Wasser gefüllt sind. Wenn du heftig kreiselst, kommt das Wasser darin in Schwung. Wenn du wieder still stehst, dreht es sich zunächst noch weiter! Dein Ohr meldet daher immer noch: „Da dreht sich was." Dein Auge dagegen sagt: „Du stehst still." Die Folge von dem Chaos: Dir ist schwindelig ...

Die unmöglichen Gabeln

Du brauchst:

- zwei Kuchengabeln
- eine Münze
- ein Glas

Stecke die Münze zwischen die zwei Gabeln. Dann legst du diese Konstruktion vorsichtig auf den Rand eines Glases. Du brauchst dazu ganz ruhige Hände.

Was passiert?

Es ist kaum zu glauben – aber die Gabeln und die Münze hängen neben dem Glas! Das liegt daran, dass sich der Schwerpunkt der Konstruktion genau an dem winzigen Teil der Münze befindet, der auf dem Glasrand liegt.

Balance-Artisten

Die „Himmelsleiter“ ist ein Kunststück der Artisten im „Chinesischen Staatszirkus“. Warum diese Leiter nicht umfällt? Der Trick ist, dass alle Artisten mit den Stühlen genau in der Balance sind – sodass der Schwerpunkt in der Mitte auf dem Tisch ist!

Stehaufmännchen

Du brauchst:

- Luftballons
- Tonpapier

Schneide aus Tonpapier Füße. Bohre ein kleines Loch hinein. Dann bläst du einen Luftballon auf und steckst das Mundstück durch das Loch im Papierfuß. Wirf den Luftballon hoch.

Was passiert?

Auch wenn der Ballon einen Salto macht – er landet immer auf den Füßen! Denn der schwerste Teil des Ballons wird immer am stärksten nach unten gezogen.

Tiefer gelegt!

Bei Autos, besonders bei den Formel-1-Autos, achtet man sehr darauf, den Schwerpunkt weit nach unten zu legen. Denn je tiefer der schwerste Teil des Autos ist, desto geringer wird die Gefahr, dass das Auto bei hoher Geschwindigkeit in den Kurven umkippt!

Die Überraschungskiste

Du brauchst:
- eine Dose mit Deckel
- Münzen

Befestige an einer Seite in der Dose viele Münzen und verschließe sie dann. Stelle die Dose auf die Tischkante und schiebe sie weit nach außen. Wie weit kann die Dose über die Tischkante ragen, ohne dass sie hinunterfällt?

Was passiert?
Der Schwerpunkt der Kiste verschiebt sich von der Mitte weg zu den Münzen. Die Kiste kann daher weiter über den Tischrand geschoben werden.

Ein starker Kran

Kennst du die schweren Betonplatten, die am anderen Ende eines Krans sind? Sie sorgen dafür, dass der Schwerpunkt des Krans hinter dem Führerhäuschen liegt. Wenn der Kran eine schwere Last trägt, kippt er daher nicht um!

CH OLATIER HACHEZ, BRE N

CH OLATIER HACHEZ, BRE N

Voll starke Eier

Du brauchst:

- mehrere halbe Eierschalen
- Bücher

Säubere die Eierschalen so, dass der Rand möglichst glatt ist, und lege sie mit dem Rand nach unten auf den Tisch. Nun stellst du Bücher darauf. Wie viele Bücher kannst du darauf stellen, bevor die Schalen zerbrechen?

Was passiert?

Du kannst überraschend viele Bücher nehmen – die Eierschalen-Bögen sind stark! Kaum piekst du eine Eierschale aber von innen an, geht sie ganz schnell kaputt.

Ein sicheres Zuhause

Wenn eine Henne Eier ausbrütet, ist es wichtig, dass die Eier nicht so schnell kaputtgehen. Denn sie müssen das Gewicht der Henne aushalten. Sobald die Küken aber ausschlüpfen wollen, sollte das einfach gehen – von innen lassen sich die Schalen daher schnell zerbrechen!

JOANNE K. ROWLING
Harry Potter
und die Kammer des Schreckens

Die Kraft des Bogens

Du brauchst:

- mehrere Bögen Papier
- mehrere Bücher
- Spielzeugauto oder Becher

Lege ein Papier zwischen zwei Bücherstapel und stelle ein Spielzeugauto oder einen Becher darauf. Die „Brücke“ stürzt sofort ein. Dann biegst du ein Papier zu einem Bogen und schiebst diesen Bogen unter die Papierbrücke. Nun stellst du das Gewicht wieder darauf.

Was passiert?

Die Brücke biegt sich nur ganz leicht durch – sie bleibt stehen! Das ist ein Gesetz der Statik: Das Gewicht des Spielzeugs wird auf den Bogen verteilt und der leitet das Gewicht sofort über die Seiten nach unten.

Kraftvolle Bögen

Schau dir einmal die großen gotischen Kathedralen an. Es scheint so, als ob die bunten Fenster das Gewicht der Wände tragen müssten. Das stimmt aber nicht. Denn die spitzen Bögen leiten alle Kraft um das Fenster herum in die Säulen hinein!

18

18

Ein Fall-Wettbewerb

Du brauchst:

- ein fest geknülltes Papier
- ein locker geknülltes Papier
- zwei Tischtennisbälle
- Spritze und Kanüle (Apotheke)

Fülle mithilfe der Spritze einen Tischtennisball mit Wasser. Dann stellst du dich im Freien auf einen Stuhl. Nun lass die Gegenstände von oben fallen. Was kommt zuerst unten an, was fällt am langsamsten?

Was passiert?

Eigentlich fallen alle Gegenstände gleich schnell, egal, wie schwer sie sind – wenn keine Luft im Raum ist. Aber das Papier wird von der Luft stark gebremst, vor allem das locker geknüllte. Die Tischtennisbälle werden wenig gebremst, deswegen kommen sie fast gleich schnell unten an, obwohl sie verschieden schwer sind!

Der Luftwiderstand trägt

Gleitschirmflieger nutzen den Luftwiderstand aus. Der Mensch alleine würde schnell auf den Boden fallen. Der große Luftwiderstand des Gleitschirms jedoch bremst den Fall so stark ab, dass der Gleitschirm nur ganz langsam zur Erde sinkt.

Vorwärts wird rückwärts

Du brauchst:
- eine Lokomotive mit Elektromotor
- eine Schiene
- drei runde Stifte

Lege die Schiene auf die Bleistifte. Dann setzt du die Lok darauf, wie auf dem oberen Bild zu sehen ist. Schalte nun die Lok ein.

Was passiert?
Die Lok fährt kaum vorwärts, aber die Schienen fliegen mit Schwung nach hinten! Denn: „Jede Bewegung bringt eine entgegengesetzte Bewegung mit sich!“ Das ist ein physikalisches Gesetz!

Feste Schrauben

Hast du dir schon einmal überlegt, warum Schienen so tief im Boden verankert sind? Dieser Versuch zeigt den Hauptgrund dafür: Sie würden sonst nämlich nach hinten wegfliegen!

BRIO

BRIO

Eine tolle Rakete

Du brauchst:

- einen Luftballon
- einen Trinkhalm
- Klebefilm
- Schnur

Führe die Schnur durch den Trinkhalm und befestige ein Ende der Schnur an einer Türklinke. Dann bläst du einen Ballon auf (nicht zuknoten!) und klebst den Trinkhalm fest. Jetzt musst du die Schnur festhalten – und den Ballon loslassen.

Was passiert?

Die Luft bläst nach hinten weg – und durch die Gegenbewegung (erinnere dich an das Experiment mit der Lokomotive!) wird der Ballon nach vorne geschossen!

Unbekannter Raketenantrieb

Viele Leute meinen, dass die Rakete startet, weil sie sich vom Boden abdrückt. Das stimmt aber nicht: Die Rakete fliegt wegen der Kraft, die gegen die Explosion wirkt. Zum Beweis: Raketen fliegen sogar im luftleeren Raum – deswegen werden sie auch im Weltall gezündet!

Am langen Hebel

Du brauchst:

- ein langes Lineal
- einen Stift
- Gewichte

Lege das Lineal so auf den Stift, dass ein Ende des Lineals länger ist als das andere. Dann stellst du zunächst ein Gewicht auf das lange Ende und versuchst, das Lineal am kurzen Ende herunterzudrücken. Dann stellst du das Gewicht auf das kurze Ende – und drückst noch einmal.

Was passiert?

Wenn sich das Gewicht am langen Ende befindet, ist es ganz schön schwer, das Lineal zu kippen. Ist es jedoch am kurzen Ende, ist es ganz einfach!

Das Geheimnis der Wippe

Du kennst dieses Prinzip gewiss von der Spielplatz-Wippe. Wenn du mit einem Erwachsenen auf den normalen Sitzen der Wippen sitzt, klappt es nicht. Aber wenn der Erwachsene näher zur Mitte rutscht, könnt ihr wippen – denn dann bist du am längeren Ende!

Wasser steht Kopf

Du brauchst:

- einen Eimer mit Henkel

Fülle den Eimer mit wenig Wasser. Dann schleuderst du den Eimer mit viel Schwung im Kreis herum. Führe diesen Versuch unbedingt nur im Freien durch!

Was passiert?

Wird der Eimer schnell genug geschleudert, so bleibt das Wasser im Eimer und fließt nicht heraus. Denn die Fliehkraft zieht das Wasser und den Eimer von dir weg.

Warum fallen wir nicht aus dem Looping raus?

Die Geschwindigkeit des Karussells drückt uns fest in den Sitz. Je schneller die Wagen sind, desto größer ist diese Fliehkraft. Und diese Kraft ist größer als die Erdanziehungskraft. Deswegen fallen wir nicht aus dem Looping raus.

Ein Seiltänzer-Clown

Du brauchst:

- einen Clown aus Papier
- zwei 10-Cent-Stücke
- eine Schnur

Bastle aus Papier einen Clown, so wie auf dem Foto zu sehen ist. Klebe ihm zwei Münzen an die Hände. Nun kannst du ihn mit dem Kinn auf eine gespannte Schnur setzen.

Was passiert?

Der Clown kippt nicht um! Du kannst ihn sogar langsam die Schnur abwärts hüpfen lassen. Denn sein größtes Gewicht, sein Schwerpunkt, liegt tief unterhalb der Schnur in seinen Händen!

Warum halten Seiltänzer eine Stange in den Händen?

Alle Hochseil-Artisten halten eine lange Stange in den Händen. So verlegen sie ihren Schwerpunkt tiefer – und verteilen das Gewicht weiter an die Seiten. Dadurch stehen sie stabiler auf dem Seil. Aus dem gleichen Grund streckst du auch die Arme aus, wenn du balancierst!

Ein Wasser-Motor

Du brauchst:
- einen Jogurtbecher
- zwei Trinkhalme mit Knick
- Schnur
- Knete

Bohre nahe dem Boden zwei gegenüberliegende Löcher in den Jogurtbecher. Schneide die biegsamen Teile der Trinkhalme ab und stecke sie in die Löcher. Dichte die Löcher mit Knete ab. Nun befestigst du den Becher mit Schnur an einem Wasserhahn und drehst das Wasser auf.

Was passiert?
Das Wasser tritt in einer Richtung aus und drückt dabei die Halme in die andere Richtung. Und der Becher dreht sich!

Das Steuerrad des Kraken

Der Krake hat in seinem Körper einen Hohlraum, der mit Wasser gefüllt ist. Wenn er diesen zusammenpresst, drückt er das Wasser durch ein kleines Loch hinaus und schießt vorwärts. Das kleine Austrittsloch lässt sich zu allen Seiten verstellen. So verändert der Krake seine Schwimmrichtung.

Auf Rollen

Du brauchst:

- ein Buch
- runde Bleistifte
- einen Gummiring
- Klebestreifen

Klebe den Gummiring auf das Buch und versuche, es am Gummi über den Tisch zu ziehen. Klappt das? Wie lange wird das Gummi dabei? Nun legst du die Stifte unter das Buch und versuchst das Ganze noch einmal. Wie sehr dehnt sich das Gummi nun?

Was passiert?

Wenn das Buch direkt auf dem Tisch liegt, bremst die Reibung zwischen Buch und Tisch. Das Gummi wird sehr lange. Wenn die Stifte darunter liegen, gibt es nur wenig Reibung – die Roll-Reibung. Und plötzlich lässt sich das Buch ganz leicht ziehen!

Warum rollt das Fahrrad?

Schlechte Fahrräder brauchen viel Kraft beim Treten. Gute Fahrräder dagegen rollen leicht. Ein Grund dafür sind gute Kugellager, zum Beispiel im Tretlager, dort, wo die Pedale angebracht sind. Je besser das Kugellager ist, desto geringer die Reibung – und umso leichter rollt das Fahrrad!

DONALD DUCK
50 JAHRE
UND KEIN BISSCHEN LEISE
Unipart

DONALD DUCK
50 JAHRE
UND KEIN BISSCHEN LEISE
Unipart

Das schnittfeste Papier

Du brauchst:

- eine Kartoffel
- ein Messer
- ein Blatt Papier

Schlage das Papier um die scharfe Kante des Messers. Dann drückst du mit dem Messer durch eine Kartoffel.

Was passiert?

Der Druck der Klinge wird über das Papier an die Kartoffel weitergegeben. Diese gibt nach, weil sie weicher ist als das Papier: Die Kartoffel wird durchschnitten, das Papier bliebt heil!

Der Nagel in der Wand

Du kannst einen Nagel nur dann in die Wand schlagen, wenn der Nagel härter ist als die Mauer. Jeder Heimwerker kennt das Problem, wenn eine Betonmauer zu stark ist: Der Nagel dringt keinen Millimeter in die Wand ein, sondern wird zu einer „Wackelschlange".

Es zieht und flieht

Du brauchst:

- einen Jogurtbecher mit Murmeln
- zwei Klebefilm-Ringe
- Schnur

Binde den Jogurtbecher an die Schnur. Ziehe die Schnur durch einen Klebefilm-Ring und befestige am anderen Ende den zweiten Klebefilm-Ring. Dann stellst du den Becher auf den Tisch und hältst den ersten Ring in der Hand. Nun beginnst du, den anderen Ring im Kreis zu schwingen, schneller und schneller.

Was passiert?

Der äußere Kebefilm-Ring will immer weiter weg und zieht dabei langsam den Jogurtbecher nach oben. Wenn alles im Gleichgewicht ist, schwingt der volle Ring gerade so stark, dass der Jogurtbecher schwebt.

Unser Sonnensystem

Die Planeten kreisen mit großer Geschwindigkeit um die Sonne. Gleichzeitig werden sie von der Sonne angezogen. Das ganze System befindet sich im perfekten Gleichgewicht. Die Planeten drehen so schnell, dass sie nicht zur Sonne gezogen werden – aber nicht zu schnell, sonst würden sie aus dem Sonnensystem hinausgeschleudert werden.

PROFESSIONAL Portrait Lighting

Techniques and Images from Master Photographers

Michelle Perkins

Amherst Media, Inc. ■ Buffalo, NY

ABOUT THE FRONT COVER—Would you believe this image was lit using white kitchen garbage bags for diffusion? Michael Biondo created this photograph with a Canon 1ds Mark II camera. For more, see pages 45–48.

Front cover photograph by Michael Biondo. Back cover photographs by George Simian (left) and Cordetta Spells (right). All other images by the photographers profiled in each respective chapter.

Published by:
Amherst Media, Inc.
P.O. Box 586
Buffalo, N.Y. 14226
Fax: 716-874-4508
www.AmherstMedia.com

Publisher: Craig Alesse
Assistant Editor: Barbara A. Lynch-Johnt
Editorial Assitance from: Carey Ann Maines

ISBN: 1-58428-190-1
Library of Congress Card Catalog Number: 2005937372

Printed in Korea.
10 9 8 7 6 5 4 3 2 1

TABLE OF CONTENTS

INTRODUCTION

Amherst Media's Pro Photo Workshop™ series is designed to provide professional photographers (and aspiring professionals) with an inside look at the working practices of leaders in the industry. In each chapter, you'll find a detailed look at the way one photographer has conquered the challenges of his or her market to build a successful business while still producing images that are creative and personally satisfying.

In this particular volume, the challenge in question is portrait lighting. As you'll see, each of the profiled photographers approaches this in a unique way, based on their personal tastes, the requirements and tastes of their clients, the realities of the location, and much more. But in the end, their goal is almost always the same: to create a portrait that says something about the subject and satisfies—hopefully even thrills—their client.

From commercial imaging, to fashion photography, to traditional portraiture, the looks that are in style and the means used to achieve them (especially with the advent of digital imaging) are constantly evolving. In this book, you'll see how some of the most successful photographers around are using these changes to enhance their work and produce ever more appealing and marketable images.

Thanks go out to the photographers who generously contributed their images, time, and knowledge to create this book. Without them, it wouldn't have been possible.

1. STEPHEN A. DANTZIG

Master the Physics

Stephen Dantzig's complete fascination with lighting began when his high-school photography class had a two-week lesson on studio lighting. "If there is such a thing as 'love at first experience,' then this was it," he says. "I was instantly enthralled with using light and spent my senior year putting together my first portfolio."

Looking back, he says he realizes that those photos were both pretty wonderful . . . and pretty bad. They were wonderful because he was "doing it"—slowly learning about light and doing the best he could at the time. "They were also, comparatively, pretty bad," he says, "because, during those formative years, I didn't know that understanding light and learning how to use it is a process—sometimes a *long* and *frustrating* process!"

As he attended classes, read books, and continued to hone his skills behind the camera, Stephen made it a point to study light. "I watched how the light streaming in the window would change over the course of a three-hour lecture. I looked at outdoor scenes and guessed what the various exposures would be in different spots."

"One of my most critical experiences," he says, "was when I worked as an apprentice for five years with my good friend, Bill Higgins. I would shoot a job, show Bill the results, and then hear the brutally honest critique. There were many times when I asked how to fix the problem only to hear, 'That's your job—figure it out!'" Higgins would drop a hint, but it was ultimately up to Stephen to think the problem through. He wasn't being taught specific techniques; rather, he was being taught to think about the *processes* and *laws* that govern photography. Later, Stephen discovered the wisdom of this; when he took more advanced seminars, he was readily able to understand what was being taught and exactly how to apply it.

Having benefitted so greatly from this approach, it's now the strategy he recommends to all photographers looking to gain a greater mastery of light: learn the physics and master the tools. Armed with this

STEPHEN DANTZIG, PSY.D. is a highly esteemed professional photographer and writer who specializes in fashion, beauty, and corporate photography. His articles and images have appeared in notable national magazines such as *Rangefinder, Studio Photography and Design,* and *Professional Photographer*. He is also the author of *Lighting Techniques for Fashion and Glamour Photography* and *Master Lighting Techniques for Outdoor & Location Digital Portrait Photography,* both from Amherst Media. Additionally, Stephen's engaging portraits have graced the covers of over twenty magazines. Stephen is the recipient of twenty-one Awards of Merit from the Professional Photographers of Los Angeles County. He also holds a doctorate degree in psychology from Rutgers University. He currently resides in Honolulu, HI. To learn more about Stephen and to view more of his images, or buy signed copies of his books, visit www.dantzigphotography.com.

knowledge, you'll be prepared to produce the looks you want and solve any problems that may arise.

The images and techniques presented in this chapter illustrate some of the fundamental concepts of lighting—skills that are required for creating outstanding portraits.

QUALITY OF LIGHT

The quality of light refers to how harsh or soft the light looks in your image. There are three characteristics that determine the quality of light used in a photograph. "Harsh lighting is characterized by long, deep shadows, high contrast, and sharp edge

7-INCH REFLECTOR PARABOLIC SPOT

SMALL SILVER UMBRELLA

SMALL STRIPDOME

MEDIUM STRIPDOME

LARGE LITEDOME

EXTRA-LARGE LITEDOME

ABOVE—To a large degree, the quality of light depends on the size of the light source, as shown in this sequence of images. **FACING PAGE**—For this pensive image of Aiko, the main light was a 30x40-inch soft box placed close and overhead with a California Sunbounce placed below her to provide the fill. The result is clean, open, and shadowless lighting that accentuates the face and cosmetics. The soft-focus effect was created in Photoshop. Mayumi Kondo styled Aiko's hair and makeup.

transfer," says Stephen. "Soft lighting, on the other hand, is characterized by lower contrast and faint shadows." Portrait photography is an area where you often see a lot of soft lighting, but photographers alter the quality of the light they use depending upon the desired effect.

SIZE OF THE SOURCE

To a large degree, the quality of light depends on the size of the light source. The images on the previous page show the effect of the size of the light source on the quality of the light. Stephen notes, "Aiko has a petite nose, but it still casts a deep shadow when smaller light sources are used. Perhaps even more telling is the intensity of the specular highlight created by the different size lights. The spotlight and umbrella create small and bright highlights on Aiko's cheek and nose. The two soft boxes produce soft and even highlights that blend smoothly with the skin."

DISTANCE TO THE SUBJECT

The distance between the light source and the subject also impacts the results the light will produce. "The sun is a huge source of light," notes Stephen, "but unless we modify the light somehow, it acts as a pinpoint light because it is so far away from us." When the sun's light is scattered through clouds or through man-made diffusers, it takes on a much softer quality. In the studio, a large soft box that creates subtle, soft shadows when placed three feet from the model will cast deeper, darker shadows as it is moved farther from the subject.

So how do you determine the best placement of a light? "Every light source has an 'ideal' distance that allows you to maximize its design," says Stephen. "In the case of a rectangular soft box, you use the Pythagorean theorem to determine the distance that will optimize the contrast of the box while maintaining its quality of light."

To determine this, draw an imaginary diagonal line from one corner of the soft box to the other, creating two right triangles, as seen in the diagram to the right. The theoretical ideal distance would be the hypotenuse of the right triangle. The Pythagorean theorem tells us that the hypotenuse (C) is obtainable via the following equation:

$$A^2 + B^2 = C^2$$

Let's assume that A=40 inches and B=30 inches for a fairly standard 30x40-inch soft box. A^2=1600 (40x40), and B^2=900 (30x30), so C^2=2500 (1600 + 900). The hypotenuse, C, is determined by taking the square root of 2500, which is 50 inches. Therefore, theoretical ideal placement for a 30x40-inch soft box is 50 inches from the subject.

"Thankfully," says Stephen, "there is a much simpler and significantly less scientific way to determine the 'ideal' placement of a light source: pull the light back a good distance from your subject. Slowly move it closer. There will be a spot where the light will suddenly 'pop' off your subject's face—and that is the ideal distance for your light."

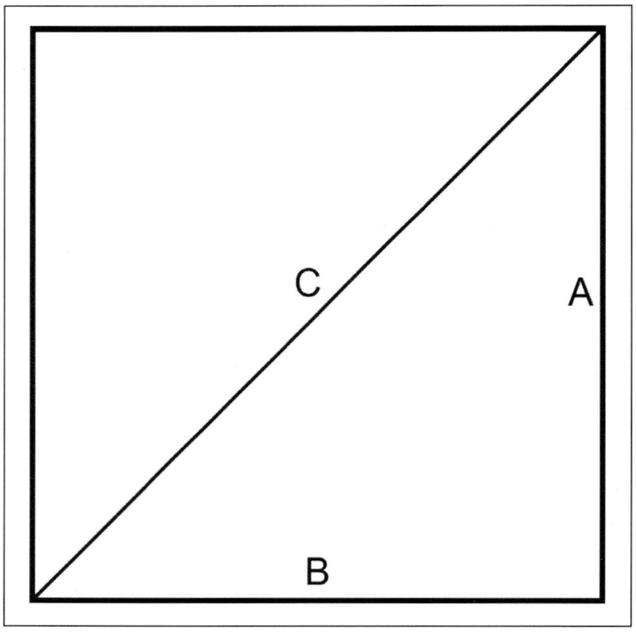

ABOVE—The "ideal" placement of any light source is obtainable through the Pythagorean theorem. However, you can also determine the ideal spot by watching your subject's face as you slowly bring the light closer to your subject. His or her face will "pop" with light at the ideal spot. This technique might not be as scientific, but it will work in a pinch! **FACING PAGE**—A single soft box can be an effective lighting tool for portraiture or fashion photography. The exact placement and size of the soft box will determine the final lighting effect. Tara Rice was lit with a single Photoflex Large LiteDome with a silver card placed on the opposite side of her face for a reflected fill source.

ABOVE AND FACING PAGE—These images showcase the different effects that can be obtained with different hair lights. They also show how one backdrop can be effectively turned into several backdrops by using colored gels to light it—or by choosing to let the backdrop stay neutral. Michele Ivey's hair (above left) was lit with a soft box overhead while the off-white backdrop was lit to stay off-white. The glamorous beauty shot of Aiko (facing page) shows the use of StripDomes as hair lights. Drinda's hair (above right) was lit with spotlights. The backdrop used for the image of Drinda was a brownish-green muslin lit with colored gels. Michele and Drinda's hair and makeup were done by Heidi Kahlenberg, while Mayumi Kondo styled the look for Aiko.

ADDING A HAIR LIGHT

"The types and positions of my hair lights vary from job to job," says Dantzig. "Some days I use a medium soft box overhead. Other times I use StripDomes on either side of the model to emphasize her hair." With a smaller light source (like a grid spot), Dantzig typically balances the hair light with the main light. "You will have to play with these values," he says. "I have found that as I increase the size of the hair light, I need to slightly increase its intensity to get the luminosity that I want. Conversely, in the digital world, you may need to meter the hair light at less than your main lights, depending upon the size of the hair light. Each combination may be a little different, so play with the values until you are comfortable with your results."

LIGHTING THE BACKDROP

"The choice of a backdrop—and how to light it—is a critical, yet often overlooked part of your set," says Dantzig. "How you light your backdrop depends on how light or dark you want it in relation to your main light. If you are lighting a colored backdrop (like a colored seamless), add a colored gel over your light source to match the hue of the backdrop; otherwise you risk washing out its natural colors."

OUTDOOR LIGHTING

As a photographer who lives and works in scenic Hawaii, many of Dantzig's assignments call for him to shoot outdoors. While this presents some additional challenges, his objectives remain the same: control the light to create a flattering portrait.

ABOVE AND FACING PAGE—Using outdoor locations can add a lot of variety to your images. It can also give you the opportunity to employ studio lighting outdoors. In the image above, a StripDome was used as the main light. In the image on the facing page, a spotlight was used. The key to using these lights outdoors is balancing them with the existing light for a natural appearance.

"Controlling and manipulating light is the technical key to creating a pleasing and saleable professional portrait," says Dantzig. "Outdoor portraiture involves the use and control of one constant light source: the sun. Other light sources may be brought in to accent or even override the sunlight, but its presence is always a factor."

Unfortunately, direct overhead sunlight produces images that are extremely contrasty with bright highlights and deep, dark shadows. The results are ugly (at best) with negative film and are just about useless with digital capture, because the range from highlight to shadow is beyond what can currently be captured with digital technology. Just as in the studio, however, softening the light comes down to adjusting the size of the source relative to the subject and bringing the source closer to the subject.

"There are times when nature provides her own diffuser," says Dantzig. "A cloud cover can create soft and beautiful light that is easy to work with. However, it is difficult to rely on overcast or cloudy days to give you enough contrast to create a successful image. Those conditions often produce flat and boring light. You'll be better off shooting on a sunny day and finding ways to increase the size of your light source by using the environment and/or artificial means."

The easiest way to increase the size of your light is to find open shade. When the light illuminating your subject is diffused by trees, an overhang, etc., it

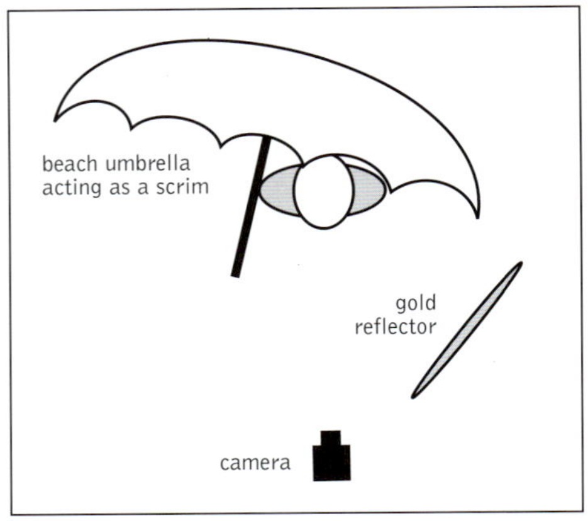

Extreme care must be taken in the positioning of the scrim if it is going to be this close to your subject; it is very easy to create a heavily backlit scene resulting in flare and loss of image quality.

becomes indirect and diffused (and therefore larger and softer than the direct light), but it still maintains some direction.

"It can be difficult to determine the direction of the light in open shade, but it is necessary to study the light in order to meter the scene properly," notes Dantzig. "Your base exposure is the highlight side of your subject's face. Everything else has to fall within plus or minus 2 to 2½ stops. Once the direction of light and your metering point is established, you can decide how to create the lighting ratio you want. You may need to move your subject closer to the edge of the shade, allowing more of the unfiltered light to illuminate the highlights. Conversely, the inverse square law dictates that the highlights will fade as you move your subject deeper into the shade."

Of course, there are many situations when you will want to modify the existing light but will either not have access to open shade or the shaded areas will not work for the image you have in mind. In such situations, scrims (translucent fabric stretched over a frame) can be used to provide beautifully soft light in almost any situation. Sunlight hits the scrim and turns it into a light source as large as the piece of fabric used. The light that passes through the fabric is what illuminates your subject. "The light is much softer and diffused, but the direction needed to create a three-dimensional feel is maintained," says Dantzig.

Using a scrim rather than open shade will also affect the color temperature of the light. "Open shade raises the color temperature (resulting in a bluish shift) and white fabric will lower the color temperature of the light (resulting in an amber cast)," says Dantzig. "I personally like a warmer tone in my images, so I like using scrims."

CONCLUSION

"The only constant in the ever-evolving field of photography is light," says Dantzig. "It acts in extremely predictable and generally controllable ways." Mastering the laws that control light is therefore an invaluable skill—and one that you can depend on regardless of the other changes in the field.

2. JEFF SMITH

Corrective Lighting Makes the Sale

Jeff Smith is an acclaimed portrait photographer who specializes in senior portraits. Yet even when working with these subjects—people who are probably the slimmest and most attractive they will ever be—he approaches each shoot with one question in mind: What would this person *not* want to see in his or her portrait?

It may seem like a negative way to approach a session, but Jeff actually has his bottom line in mind. After all, regardless of the style, the props, or the composition, people ultimately *buy* portraits that make them look *good*. The easiest way to accomplish that goal is to identify potential problem areas and minimize or disguise them. And keep this in mind: whether the appearance issues in question are real or imagined from the *photographer's* point of view, it's the *client's* point of view that matters. Even if you think her nose looks just fine, if a woman feels it's too big, you'd better de-emphasize it in her portrait if you want to make the sale.

As a result of this approach, Jeff's lighting strategy contradicts the staid notion that light is the photographer's "paint brush." Corrective lighting, he

Jeff Smith's portrait photography business bases its success on creating flattering portraits of real people—and carefully crafted lighting is an integral part of the process.

JEFF SMITH is an award-winning senior photographer from Fresno, CA. He owns and operates two studios in Central California and is well recognized as a speaker on lighting and senior photography. He is the author of *Corrective Lighting, Posing, and Retouching for Digital Photographers* (Amherst Media, 2005), *Senior Contracts* (self-published), and *Outdoor and Location Portrait Photography* (Amherst Media, 2003). He can be reached via his web site: www.jeffsmithphoto.com.

ABOVE AND FACING PAGE—By shooting his portraits in a dark area, Jeff ensures that no light is bounced off the walls or items in the room. This means he can put light and shadow exactly where he wants it and not have it diminished by light reflected from the surroundings.

notes, is actually much more about shadow. He feels it's the control of shadow, more than any other factor, that sets the work of skilled professionals apart from the "factory" portraits created in mall and department-store photo studios.

Says Jeff, "Any student photographer with two lights and a meter can create a decent portrait—just put the main light at a 45-degree angle to the subject and place the other light behind the camera. Set the lights so the main light is two stops brighter than the light behind the camera, stick a diffusion filter on the lens, and there you have it! I have just taught everyone with any knowledge of photography to create a realistic portrait with the appearance of a third dimension."

Naturally, this is precisely the lighting setup that most mall studios use—it's easy to learn, easy to use and, for a huge segment of the buying public, acceptable for a cheap portrait. Unfortunately, it's also the lighting setup that many *professional* studios use. "While clients will accept this type of portrait if they are getting it cheap," says Jeff, "they are not going to pay a professional studio's price for something they could get at the mall for much less." Professionals need to deliver more than an "acceptable" portrait.

This is where shadow comes in; it is shadow that gives a portrait dimension, and it is shadow that lets Jeff disguise his clients' flaws—flaws they aren't paying to see (or more to the point, flaws they won't *pay for* if they *do see*).

In the basic "mall lighting" setup described earlier, this degree of control is impossible. Combine a large main light and a fill light with the white walls of most studios and you have light bouncing around off of everything. As a result, Jeff has tailored his lighting techniques and his studio itself to combat these obstacles.

THE STUDIO

Although his studio features several camera areas, it's the low-key area where he makes the most of his skills with corrective lighting. "In this area," he says, "we've worked to eliminate features that reduce the control you have over your lighting. Thus, the entire area is black—walls, floor, etc. Even the props and furniture are all black or very dark. This ensures that no light is bounced off the walls or items in the room, so I can put shadow exactly where I want it and not have it diminished by the surroundings."

THE MAIN LIGHT

The main light that Jeff uses with corrective lighting is a 24x36-inch soft box with a recessed front panel and louvers. The size of the box allows him to get a softer light when the box is placed close to the subject, but he can also make the light more contrasty by pulling it back just a little. The louvers on Jeff's main light control the light from side to side, preventing light rays from spilling out of the side of the box. To control light from the top and bottom of the box, you must either feather the light or use a gobo to block the light from hitting areas that you want to keep in shadow.

Jeff notes that there are some differences to be aware of when working with smaller light sources that produce more contrasty light. First, you have to watch out for shadows in unwanted places. You can get some harsh shadows on the unlit side of the nose, for example. Second, small light sources can't be

The main light that Jeff uses with corrective lighting is a 24x36-inch soft box with a recessed front panel and louvers.

feathered like large ones; with large light sources that don't have a recessed front, you can use just the edge of the light to soften the light or cut down on the output. If you try that with a small louvered box, you will have light falloff on the highlight side of the face.

THE FILL LIGHT

To add fill light only where it is wanted, Jeff uses a reflector. "When I was learning photography, I was taught, like all young photographers, that you use a flash to fill the shadow," says Jeff. "You put this enormous light source at the back wall of the camera room, and it literally fills your entire camera room to a certain level of light. I was then instructed that to avoid flat lighting you would use a ratio between the main light and fill of 3:1 without diffusion, and 4:1 with diffusion."

"I worked with this for quite some time," he recalls. "It wasn't until a young African-American woman came into my studio and talked with me about doing her portraits that I saw a problem. She asked me if I had ever photographed an African-American person before. I thought for a minute and realized that I never had. She explained that she had had her portraits taken several times, at several places, and they just didn't look right. She said they had very heavy shadows. When she said this, I suddenly realized how limiting the use of fill flash was. My first thought was, 'Wait a minute, I use a 3:1 or 4:1 ratio, but that is for a light skin tone. What ratio do I use for all the other shades of skin?'"

Jeff did the session, but he used a reflector for fill so he could see the results he was achieving—and see them on *her* face, with *her* skin tone, and *her* facial structure. She loved the portraits, and he learned a lesson. "You can know what the ratio of lighting is by metering," he says, "but when you use a flash fill you will never know what the 'perfect' ratio of light is for each individual's skin tone and facial structure."

"In this country we have a variety of people, with different shades of skin, different facial structures, and (need I point out?) different problems and flaws to hide," says Jeff. "The only way to evaluate the right amount of fill is to see it with your own eyes."

THE SEPARATION LIGHT

Because corrective lighting relies on higher contrast lighting, you must use separation—but only in the areas of your client you want separated. In Jeff's por-

TROXEL

traits, he uses a small strip light overhead as a hair light. This light is aimed back toward the camera and meters one stop less than the main light. This provides a soft highlight on the top of the subject's hair and shoulders.

For clients with long hair, Jeff uses two lights behind the subject. Each is placed at a 45-degree angle to the subject. These lights are set to meter at the same reading as the main light for blond hair or lighter clothing, or to one stop more than the main light reading for black hair and dark clothing. These accent lights are also fitted with barndoors to keep the light from hitting an area of the subject he does not want to illuminate.

POSITIONING THE LIGHTS

"The angle of the main light is always determined by the orientation of the subject's nose," says Jeff. "With the subject's nose pointed directly at the camera, the main light should be at approximately a 45-degree angle to the camera." To add shadow or bring out more facial structure, you may increase the angle of the light, but this is the angle at which most portraits will be taken. "The great thing is that the light always stays at approximately a 45-degree angle to where the nose is pointing—even when you go to a profile," Jeff notes.

Once the main light is in position, Jeff decides how much of the shadow area needs to be filled. He may start with no fill at all. If the portrait looks great, he won't add any fill. "Somewhere along the line, you were probably told, like I was, that you have to see some detail in the shadow area," he says. "Wrong! If a shadow that goes black is what makes your subject look his best, then that is the perfect lighting to use on that individual client."

Most of the time, however, some fill is necessary to bring the shadows to a printable level. Jeff starts with the reflector far away from the subject, then moves it progressively closer until he gets the effect he wants. He tends to use a soft silver reflector and pulls it out farther than he would if he were using a white one.

With the main light and fill reflector in place, separating the subject from the background is the next step. "Remember," he says, "no separation from the background means no point of reference behind the subject. No point of reference behind or in front of your subject means no depth in the portrait." Again, Jeff says there are no rules. You have just one objec-

Use separation light to accent only the parts of the client you want to draw attention to. Three variations are shown here, with separation light on the lower body (left), upper body (center), and head and shoulders (right).

tive, and that is to make your client look as good as possible.

Jeff begins with the hair. For this, a strip light attached to the ceiling gives a soft separation to the hair and shoulders when the light is metered at one stop less than the main light. To finish the separation, he adds a light behind the subject and aimed directly toward the hair. This creates an intense rim light all the way around the hair. This meters from one stop more than the main light for blond hair to three stops more than the main for brunette or black hair. "This type of portrait is simple," says Jeff, "but very salable because it gives any client a version of reality they can live with."

Separation becomes a critical issue when the client has a weight issue. "The idea," says Jeff, "is that you don't want to see a perfect outline of the body in a problem area. With the background light low and the subject standing in dark clothes against a dark background, you separate the hips and thighs (areas you know your client will worry about looking large). Raising the background light to waist height will separate the waistline and chest, making them more noticeable. Elevate the separation light to the height of the shoulders, and only the head and shoulders will be separated, leaving the body to blend with the background."

The greater the intensity of the background light, the more attention it draws to whatever part of the body it is separating—unless the subject is wearing lighter-colored clothing. Often a client will select a dark background and want to wear lighter-colored clothing with it. In this situation, by increasing the background light to match the brighter tone of the outfit, you will actually lessen the attention drawn to this area. By coordinating the tone of the clothes and the background (whether dark on dark or light on light), you can bring the focus of the portrait away from the person's body and to his or her face. If, on the other hand, you create contrast between the clothing and background, you will attract attention to the subject's body.

When weight is a big issue and the subject has long hair, Jeff leaves the background as dark as possible and puts a light directly behind the subject, facing toward the camera, to give the hair an intense rim light all around the edges. This draws the attention directly to the facial area and keeps the viewer's eye away from the shoulders, arms, and upper body.

When clothing selection, background selection, posing, and lighting all come together, the result is a portrait that flatters the subject and has lasting appeal.

LIGHTING THE FULL-LENGTH POSE

Since senior portraits became a hot topic in the early 1980s, lecturers, authors, and educators have hailed the offering of full-length portraits as one of the best ways to set your studio apart from the contracted studios. Jeff, however, feels that the full- or three-quarter-length pose has been oversimplified and its importance overstated. "I have never seen one of those photographer/lecturers stroll out with a model who is five-feet tall with a tummy bulge and short legs," he says. "Therefore, my first rule of full- or

three-quarter-length poses is that if there is any reason not to do them, then don't." Using corrective lighting, selecting the proper background, and making good clothing choices can do a lot to enhance a person's appearance, but if the subject has significant problems (a serious weight issue, large scars from burns, etc.), no amount of enhancements can produce a salable portrait in a full-length pose.

Low-Key Setups. Corrective lighting for a full- or three-quarter-length pose relies heavily on using light's falloff to act as a vignette, thereby throwing certain problem areas into complete darkness and not allowing the camera to record the problems or flaws in those areas. The second lighting tool for correction is one that has already been noted: separation. By selecting the area of the body you wish to separate from the background, you determine which area of the body the viewer's eye will be drawn to.

Surprisingly, in this low-key setup, Jeff sticks to the same main light for longer portraits that he uses for head-and-shoulders shots. "A 24x36-inch louvered soft box may not be the first main-light choice for the classic full-length portrait," he says, "but it is perfect for beautifully lighting the facial area and letting the rest of the subject fall completely into shadow." With this accomplished, you can proceed to add separation to the areas of the subject you feel should be seen in the portrait. This is no different for thinning a waistline than for concealing a balding head. You only separate the subject in an area that the client would want to see.

High-Key Setups. When you move to high key, lighting can do very little. In high-key portraiture, correction relies on the clothing selection, set, and pose. For this type of image, Jeff uses large light sources, then employs the other elements of the scene to hide the client's flaws. Often, something as simple as a good pose and a client's long hair can be enough to make the subject happy with the way she looks.

While very popular, high-key images are best avoided by anyone with a weight problem. With the softer, less contrasty look, faces appear heavier and bodies wider. Jeff has actually had many *thin* clients notice the difference between how wide their faces look on the high-key backgrounds as opposed to the low-key setup.

When you move to high key, lighting can do very little. However, by coordinating the tone of the clothes and the background, you can bring the focus of the portrait away from the person's body and to his or her face.

IN CLOSING

"Maybe," laughs Jeff, "there actually *is* a photographer out there somewhere who makes a good living in a portrait studio that only photographs beautiful people. If there is, I would like to shake his or her hand—and then buy the studio."

What's the "right" light? It's whatever light makes your client look his or her best.

For most photographers, portraits of gorgeous, rail-thin models aren't the images that will sustain their business and their livelihood. Instead, they will be working with average people, with average figures and faces, who want portraits that they consider flattering and attractive. That's not something you can achieve by producing images that show every inch, every pore, and every line.

"When I was a young professional and trying to define the direction of my business, I really tried to make each client look his or her best. Quite frankly, in those days I couldn't afford to lose any clients," recalls Jeff. "On one occasion, I had photographed a young senior girl who was probably 60 to 80 pounds overweight. I used a very contrasty light to have a very dark shadow, thinning the face. I used poses that hid her very large double chin from the perspective of the camera. I picked out her clothing, all of which was very dark, and used her long hair to soften the size of her shoulders and arms. At that point in time in the studio, I was both the photographer *and* the person who delivered the proofs to the client. When this girl and her mother came in to the studio and started to look at her proofs, the mother started to cry. The mother said, 'I have always told my daughter that, despite her weight, she is a beautiful young lady and these portraits show the beautiful young lady she is.' The mother gave me a hug and thanked me. This is a session I will never forget, because for the first time I understood how much a professional portrait means to our clients."

"If I could leave you with one message," says Jeff, "it would be to care about your clients—all your clients. Put the same effort into a session with a person who has obvious flaws as you do into a session with the perfect people you invite to come in for test sessions. Measure your growth on how good you can make each client look, not on your best photographs of your most beautiful clients."

3. ANDRE AMYOT

Getting Down to Business on Location

Andre Amyot is an acclaimed business-portrait photographer who is widely known for his expertise at creating on-location portraits for annual reports and corporate brochures. Of course, just saying "on-location" doesn't really begin to cover the vast array of lighting situations Andre has been faced with when creating his portraits. From construction sites and boardrooms, to airplane hangars, beaches, laboratories, restaurants, and classrooms—you name it, Andre has been there and found a way to create just the look his client needed.

EQUIPMENT

In the more than three decades since he began his career, the equipment photographers rely on has changed dramatically. Says Andre, "When I first started doing photography professionally, only daylight and tungsten flood lamps (1000 and 500 watts) were available for studio lighting. On location, we used big, heavy power packs for electronic flashes. These replaced large flash bulbs, which had lots of power but were a menace to personal safety. A friend lost half of his thumb when one of these bulbs went off as he was testing his flash gun."

Today, with the increased sensitivity of digital cameras, daylight or ambient light is more and more present in his images. He frequently drags the shutter to get the full flavor of the environment, to create motion and mood, and to get a 3-D effect in his photographs. He also uses the same technique combined with camera motion to create the dynamic images that many editors are now looking for.

Studio Systems. When it comes to selecting equipment for your studio, Andre feels that the choice is a personal one. There are many great systems available, so his best advice is to find one that suits your tastes and meets the requirements of your specialty. He suggests asking members of various professional associations for their input; they will often give you better answers than many salespeople. "One thing is for sure," he says, "it is important to buy the highest-quality equipment you can reasonably afford. It will last a lot longer than 'bargain' equipment and will require fewer repairs."

ANDRE AMYOT, also known as "PhotoCoach," is past president of Professional Photographers of Canada (PPOC) and a seasoned speaker. He has been in commercial and industrial photography for the last forty years, twenty-five of which were spent as the head of one of Montreal's largest commercial studios. He is also the author of *The Art and Techniques of Business Portrait Photography* (Amherst Media, 2003). Currently, Andre invests all of his time developing training courses for professional photographers. For more information, visit www.photocoach.com.

This photograph was created outside as part of a composite image that had the model in a dress shop looking into a large mirror and seeing her reflection as if she was outside in the wilderness. In the first test, the setting sun created a very contrasty situation and the trees in the background appeared too dark (1/125 second at f/11). To create more brilliant colors, Andre brought in a translucent panel between the model and the sun. He then took another light reading to determine a new exposure setting (1/60 second at f/8). Notice how bright the leaves are and the softness of the lighting on the model's face.

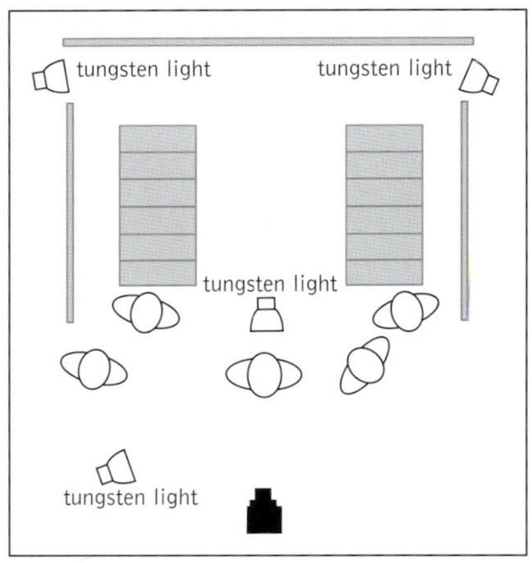

For over thirty years, Ray Vincent has been filling hotel ballrooms every week for his motivational seminars. Andre captured this energy by photographing him on a strategic spot in the very same hotel where he started his career. In addition to the ambient light, Andre used four tungsten lights: a unit to camera left, high above the subject to simulate stage lighting; an accent light behind the subject to create a halo on his hair; and, since the back screen was too dark for a proper exposure, an accent light on either side. A large skylight provided a bluish cast since the camera was set for tungsten light. Notice how the large amount of ambient light creates a feeling of depth.

"After working in a commercial studio environment for twenty-five years," says Andre, "I have settled for a lightweight, mobile system that not only gives me power but offers versatile power distribution. It also allows me to modify my light patterns with any of the many accessories available."

WORKING ON LOCATION

Corporate photographers spend many of their hours—even days—on the road. "To be honest," says Andre, "this is paradise for me. I enjoy concentrating on the job at hand without the distraction of the studio environment and telephone calls."

Making things work on location, however, takes some planning. "Once I get the specifics about an on-location assignment from my client, I fill in a chart that lists all of my equipment," says Andre. "I know that the few minutes I invest will keep me from having to come back to the studio for forgotten items and risk being late for the assignment."

When it comes to lighting, Andre relishes the challenges of working in unique situations. "Lighting

The action here called for a constant motion during the operation, so Andre decided to create a blur during the welding process. He was also trying to get the little welding spark. Ambient light was an additional consideration in the overall lighting composition, producing yellow tones that complement the blue clothing and machine. To produce the image, three lights were used. The main light was a soft box placed to camera left to cross light the subject. The fill light was a 7-inch reflector with an umbrella. This was placed to the far right of the camera behind the machine to provide separation to the subject and to backlight the machine. For an accent light, Andre used a 10-degree grid spot behind the welding area. This backlit the mist from the water and brought attention to the contact area on the gas tank. To create motion, a three-second exposure was selected. The subject was frozen with the flash. There was no need to stop production for the shot; Andre was careful to study the procedure and tripped the shutter when he could see that the proper action was taking place.

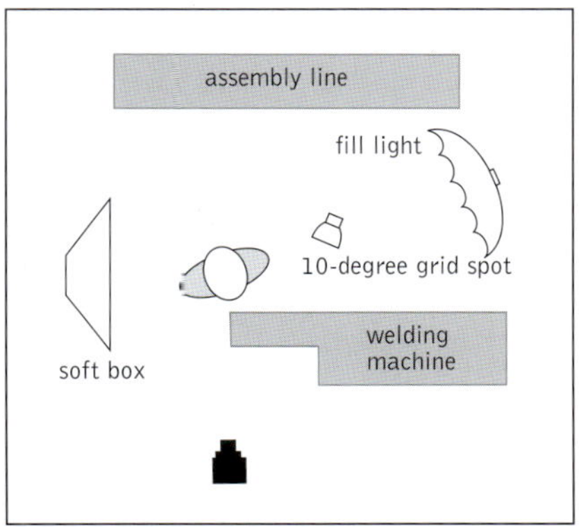

is probably the biggest challenge in location photography, since the type of ambient light coming into the scene is usually a mixture of light sources," he says.

Andre has a few tips, however, for maximizing your creativity while keeping the photo shoot safe and productive:

1. When you're on location, look into the boardroom, sneak a peek at the lobby, look for shadows created on the wall, stairwells, etc.
2. Make sure you have the proper electrical outlet. It's better to ask around before you plug your cables in the wall. Locate the circuit board before you start, in case you need to have

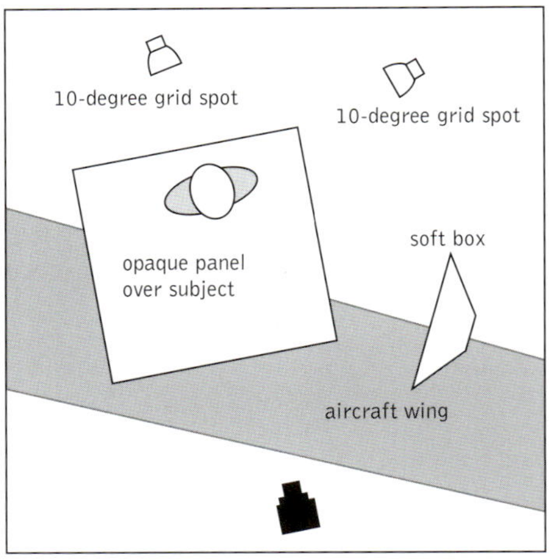

When Andre photographed his friend Gil Bedard, he wanted to show him surrounded by his life's passion: aircraft. He used a simple lighting concept that mixed ambient light and flash. A slow shutter speed was needed for the ambient light, so Andre reduced the overhead light using an opaque panel. He then shot the image from under the wing of an aircraft that was being assembled. A medium soft box was placed to camera right as the main light. A 10-degree grid spot was placed to camera right, and a backlight was also added—another 10-degree grid spot. "Working in a hangar requires safety procedures that only qualified personnel can provide," says Andre. "Power packs need to be installed at least three feet above the ground to avoid sparks causing an explosion due to fuel fumes. Proper extension cables are also required. Never, never install any electrical cables without authorization."

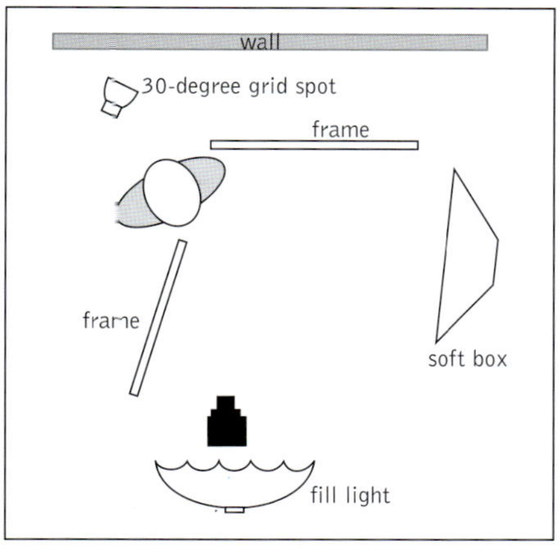

After the planned shot was created, Andre asked for a few more minutes to produce a creative variation (right). The subject and art director were both very happy with the results—and it only added ten minutes to the shoot.

access to it quickly. Ask everyone working on a computer to save their work in progress.

3. Never take for granted that a particular switch will control what you think it should.
4. Do not switch off lights without telling people. Also, let them know how long it will be before the lights are back on. Don't assume that they can work in the dark as well as you do.
5. Work slowly to avoid potential accidents. Chances are, you will not be familiar with the surroundings.

QUICK AND CREATIVE

Subject. This image of Aaron Fish (above), president and CEO of Ilco Unican, was created on his sixty-fifth birthday, and he was glowing. Andre and his assistant set up in a small boardroom and put together this concept with the advertising director. The art pieces shown in this photograph are close to Mr. Fish's heart. Simple lighting was chosen to draw the viewer's focus to the subject.

Lighting. The main light was a medium soft box (3x4 feet), placed to camera right at 90 degrees. An incident reading yielded a value of f/11 for this light. One umbrella fill light, metered at f/5.6.5 (incident reading), was placed high behind the camera for a 3:1 ratio. A backlight with a 30-degree grid spot added a third dimension, separating Mr. Fish from the background. The reflective reading was f/16.5. Since the back wall was already fairly bright in value, only a small amount of light was required. The picture frames were suspended from the ceiling at the appropriate spot.

Variations. Once the first, more traditional image was done, Andre asked Mr. Fish if he had a little more time to do another image. No change in lighting was required, Andre just repositioned the subject. "I always like to demonstrate exactly what I want my models to do," says Andre, "whether they are professional models or not."

Mr. Fish found the new approach quite creative and was very willing to try it. "The extra ten minutes it took to secure this shot was enough to solidify my position with this client," says Andre, "and it made the advertising director look good for selecting a creative and quick photographer."

HOTEL HALLWAY

Concept. As part of a recruiting campaign for a major law firm, this photograph was created in a hotel very early in the morning. The lighting concept was designed to reproduce the natural lighting that existed in this hallway. A model was asked to walk across the set to create motion in the background.

Lighting. Three light sources were used for this image. The main light was a medium soft box placed at camera left. Its exposure reading was f/3.2. A white reflector panel was placed to camera right for fill. "On the back walls," says Andre, "I wanted more light with a warmer tone, so I used two tungsten lights with amber gels." A spot reading on the wall indicated that the exposure reading was $\frac{1}{10}$ second at f/5.6.

Notice the fluorescent lights on the ceiling. They were square boxes of light, and Andre wanted to reduce the overexposure created by the light coming off them. Therefore, in each box, he removed the front and back fluorescent tubes. This reduced the value of the exposure and created contrast in the light pattern. As a bonus, it created a different perspective, making the hallway look longer.

Softening. Image manipulation was done to emphasize the softness of the background.

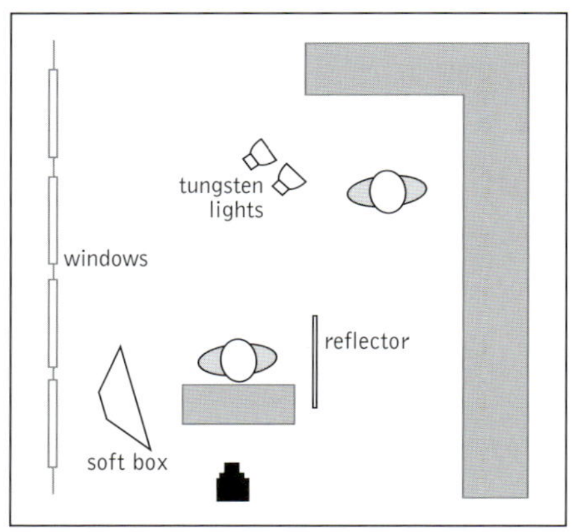

The subject of this image (above left) was seated on the arm of a chair with her arms folded on a table (top right). Overhead, Andre removed the front and back tubes from the fluorescent fixtures to prevent overexposure (center right).

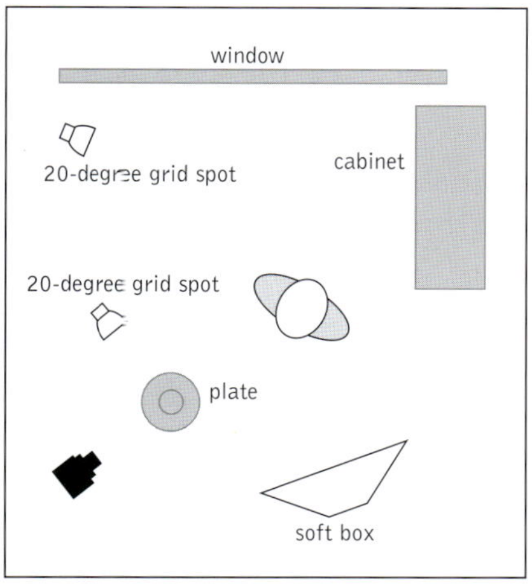

For this shot, Andre was challenged to elegantly light the subject, the food, the floral arrangement, and the background.

MIXED LIGHT

This photograph of Denise Cornellier, considered the top caterer in Montreal, was created for the front cover of *Food and Hospitality* magazine. Therefore, a vertical format was chosen, leaving enough room around and above the subject to allow for copy and the magazine headline.

Andre visited her small office the day before the shoot and decided to create her portrait in the lobby area. He asked her to prepare one of her specialties as well as a flower basket for the table decoration.

The ample ambient light in the scene was supplemented by three flash units: a medium soft box (3x4 feet) and two 20-degree grid spots. The main light (the soft box) was positioned to camera right, providing illumination for the flower basket. Andre used a gobo to prevent overexposure, since the basket was so close to the light source. The second light (a grid spot) came from camera left and produced a backlight effect on the plate. "Food always looks better when backlit," says Andre. The third light (another grid spot) was aimed inside the wood cabinet in the back because there was not enough ambient light reaching it.

Notice the amount of daylight illuminating the subject's face. It was provided by the window in the back and was calculated to give a ratio of 3:1 with the main light.

IN THE LAB

Concept. Laboratory photographs can be very dramatic. Every time Andre is asked to create an image in such an environment, he says he always dreams of "the shot."

Composition. Rarely is a setup so perfect that it requires no adjustments, and this one was no exception. Andre set up the whole thing and decided to frame the subject to focus the viewer's attention on the action. In setting up accessories, Andre recommends asking the lab director for solutions that are realistic in appearance and in color. Directions were given to the technician to hold the beaker and bottle in a believable fashion. Notice the beakers were set up very close to the lens to add depth.

Lighting. "Knowing that lab beakers show up a lot better when backlit," says Andre, "I planned to have illumination from the back wall. The frame around the image made it possible to hide my lights."

Two lights and one reflector were used for this setup. The main light used on the subject was a 20-degree grid spot. This helped to focus the light pattern on the lab technician and eliminate any front light on the beakers. Its reading was f/8.0.5. A 7-inch reflector on the back wall was used as the source of back illumination on the beakers. The reflective reading off the back wall was f/16.5. A white reflector was also positioned to open the shadows on the beakers in the foreground.

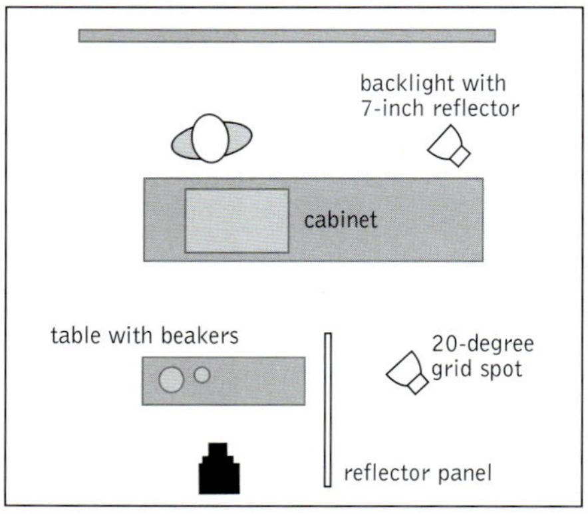

For this image created in a laboratory, Andre used a 20-degree grid spot on the subject, then backlit the beakers.

THE CONCERT HALL

Subject. Jean Marc Chaput has been a motivational speaker in Quebec for over thirty years. "I'll never forget his performance at the Place des Arts in 1977 when I was in my third year in business and much in need of a good kick in the you-know-what," says Andre. "When I told him that I wanted to do his photograph in this particular setting, his eyes perked up with enthusiasm. So I rented the concert hall for two hours."

Lighting. The main light was a medium soft box to camera left. Its exposure reading was f/5.6.5. A reflector screen was also positioned to camera right for fill. Ambient light was a major part of the concept, so Andre dragged the shutter to get it all in.

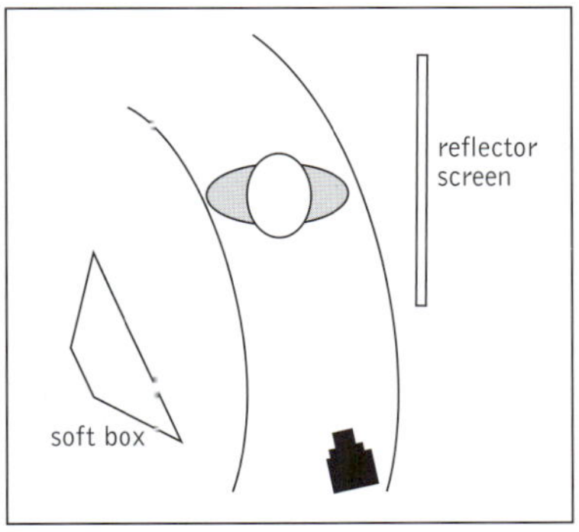

4. ROLANDO GOMEZ

Success with the Glamour Edge

For the past ten years, Rolando Gomez has been on the forefront of glamour photography, tirelessly working as a staunch defender of the often-disdained artform he is passionate about. It finally seems like people are taking notice.

Once the black sheep of the photography industry, glamour has cast off most of its "cheesecake" reputation, gotten back to its elegant Hollywood roots, and lost some of its stigma along the way. "A

RIGHT—Here, Rolando placed a Rosco #4430 green gel over the flash and white balanced his camera to its exact opposite, a Rosco #4730 magenta gel. The flash hit the model with green light, which was canceled out by the magenta. The green light did not travel to the sky, though, so the clouds took on a magenta color. (CAMERA: Olympus E-1) **FACING PAGE**—A Dyna-Lite Uni400 Jr. head with a 7-inch reflector was pointed into a 4x6-foot California Sunbounce Pro with zebra fabric. The light was placed about a foot from the reflector and aimed at a 45-degree angle into the Sunbounce reflector about two-thirds up to the top. The reflector was angled slightly down to hit the model at an angle that mimicked the setting sun. The shutter was dragged to $^1/_{25}$ second to properly expose the color of the ambient sunset. (CAMERA: Olympus E-1)

ROLANDO GOMEZ is a former combat photojournalist turned glamour photographer and the founder of the popular web site www.GarageGlamour.com—now visited by over 500,000 people each month. He has been a guest speaker at the PhotoImaging & Design Expos and Photo Plus Expos, where he drew standing-room-only crowds. His work has appeared in Playboy Special Editions products, *Studio Photography & Design* (where he is a contributing editor and writer), *Peterson's 4-Wheel Drive, Stars & Stripes,* and newspapers nationwide. Gomez is a Lexar Media Elite Photographer, a guest instructor at The Palm Beach Photographic Center and FotoFusion, and the author of *Garage Glamour: Digital Nude and Beauty Photography Made Simple* (Amherst Media, 2006). To learn more, visit www.rolandogomez.com, www.glamour1.com, or www.garageglamour.com.

good example is the recent photography of Jennifer Aniston in *Vanity Fair*," says Gomez. "The images are sexy, sensual, sultry, and seductive—but with class. That is glamour today."

Recapturing this classic legacy has also helped glamour influences slip into just about every genre of photography, from fashion and editorial work to wedding photography and portraiture. Driving this trend are magazines like *Maxim, Stuff,* and *FHM,* as well as fashion icons like Victoria's Secret, bebe, and DKNY, which have now made glamour photography practically mainstream.

The advent of digital imaging has also proven a critical factor in two ways. First, digital has allowed glamour images to be created with complete discretion—from shoot, to post-production, to printing. For interested subjects who might be sheepish about commissioning a "glamorous" image, this can be a significant inducement. "Most of my female subjects don't want to go to the local shopping mall," says Gomez. "They want to be pampered in the privacy of their own home with personalized photography."

Second, as DSLR-toting amateurs continue to steal their business, many professionals are looking for ways to recover lost revenues. This has created a renewed interest in glamour photography among studios that are looking to expand their offerings or just infuse their wedding and portrait work with a

This classic portrait with a glamour edge was illuminated by a Larson 3x4-foot soft box with a Lighttools 40-degree grid. Gomez often likes to create what he calls "suggested nude" headshots like this and often asks subjects to bring a strapless top to the shoot for this purpose. Here, the simple one-light setup created an alluring and dramatic look that keeps the attention on the model's eyes and lips—a very glamorous look. (CAMERA: Olympus E-1)

The model appears to walk on water as she strikes a pose while at edge of an infinity pool that faces the ocean. She was illuminated by a Hensel Premium Porty 1200 AS portable power pack with a Hensel Ringflash with an optional Octa Sunhaze RF90 soft box. A Rosco Bastard Amber #02 gel was placed inside the Sunhaze. (CAMERA: Olympus E-Volt E-300)

stand-out glamour edge. For many studios, this "glamourized" style has proven to be a key factor in setting them apart from others in the market.

GLAMOUR DEFINED

So what makes a portrait "glamorous?" Well, first of all, glamour is all about the subject. "Glamour photography is probably the most powerful form of photography when it comes to its essential subject," says Rolando. "Unlike fashion photography, which relies on the model to display a dress or accessories (the real subject of the photograph), in glamour photography the model is the subject of the photograph. Therefore, as photographers, it's up to us to capture that subject's inner and outer beauty. You don't need a professional model in front of your camera. Glamour photography can be applied to any subject."

The other qualities that define a glamour photo have to do with the visual idealization of the portrait's subject—creating an image that, like a classic Hollywood portrait, turns a mere mortal into a star. Rolando calls the qualities used to achieve this goal the four S's: sexiness, sultriness, sensuality, and seductiveness. Adding any one of these qualities to an image, even if it's subtle, will add a glamour edge to your portrait. Which quality you should choose and

how or to what degree it should be applied will depend on the individual image. "While we all enjoy great glamour images with sensuality and sex appeal, we must also remember that there are conservative methods for achieving a glamorous look. Don't try for an overtly sexy look in every image. Think about the intended use of the final photo. Is it for a glamour headshot or for a real-estate agent's business card? Perhaps it's a boudoir photograph for your subject's husband. As the photographer, it's up to you to discern which of the four S's is called for and how to capture it in your camera," says Rolando.

When creating glamour images, it's important to keep the final use of the portraits in mind. Here, Rolando created two very different images with one model. In the image to the left, Tiffany was photographed with an umbrella as a prop. It's a reasonably conservative type of portrait that a subject wouldn't be afraid to share with friends and family. Still, her sultry expression and direct eye contact (paired with lighting that has a dramatic edge) give the shot an appealing glamour edge. In the image below, we see a lot more skin. This type of glamour image is meant more for the subject's personal enjoyment or perhaps to be shared with her spouse or boyfriend. Rolando advises photographers to listen carefully to their models—it's the best way to determine just the kind of shots each subject is looking for. (CAMERA: Leica M-9 with Leica Digital-Modul-R back)

Noelia was photographed on location in Cozumel. The curves of her figure give the image its sex appeal. Notice how the interplay of light and shadow sculpts her figure and creates the illusion of a third dimension in the image. This is called chiaroscuro. (CAMERA: Olympus E-1)

LIGHTING

While posing plays an important role in creating the glamour look, the other key element is definitely lighting, which is used to sculpt the face and body, set the mood of the image, and keep the viewer's eyes on the subject of the portrait: the model. While a variety of techniques can be applied to create just the look you want, Rolando has a few tips.

Chiaroscuro. In Italian, chiaroscuro literally means "light" (chiaro) and "dark" (oscuro). The term describes a technique of intermixing light and dark tones to create the illusion of depth in a two-dimensional image. Today, it is used in many two-dimensional forms (like photography) to suggest a third dimension where none actually exists. Rolando uses this technique to sculpt his subject's face and body, and recommends an intuitive approach based on careful observation. "Don't pin yourself into creating exact light and dark shapes to match each other," says Rolando. "I don't ever attempt to create chiaroscuro; I watch as my model moves under the light. If I want it and don't see it, I move the lights, my model, or both, as chiaroscuro is easily created when a model is positioned at an angle to the light."

Rembrandt Lighting. The key to Rembrandt lighting is to create a triangle or diamond of light underneath the eye, usually the eye farthest from the camera lens. One side of the face is well lit from the main light source while the other side of the face gets its shape from the interaction of shadows and light—chiaroscuro. "What's important here," says Rolando, "is not how harsh or soft the shadows are, or the shape of the triangle or diamond under the eye. What matters is the illusion of depth created by the shadows. Top photographers understand that we normally see the world in a three-dimensional realm and know that digital cameras see the world in two dimensions. Because of that, they know that we need to look for those shadows—no matter how subtle they are."

A good starting point for your main light is to place it slightly higher than your subject and approx-

ABOVE—Despite the glittering accessories and abundance of red tones, your eyes still go directly to the model's face when looking at this shot. That's what makes it a glamour image rather than a fashion image (where the clothes or jewelry would be the focus of the shot). The key to directing the viewer's eye this way? Careful lighting. Rolando made sure her face was the lightest area in the frame. **FACING PAGE—**Holley was illuminated by a Hensel Beauty Dish attached to the front of a Hensel EHT3000 studio flash head, which was powered by a Hensel Vela 1500AS power pack. Since she has blond hair, Rolando was able to place her in front of a black seamless background without having to add a hair light to the image. With a darker-haired model, a hair light or reflector would normally be needed to separate the model from the background. Notice the Rembrandt lighting pattern indicated by the triangle of light on her left cheek. (CAMERA: Olympus E-1)

imately 45 degrees from the camera, but this isn't a hard-and-fast rule. "I don't carry around a compass and tape measure," says Rolando. "I look for the light and where it falls. When I see the chiaroscuro effect I want on the subject, I just have her turn her face slightly away from the light until I see the characteristic Rembrandt lighting pattern under the eye farthest from the light source."

Hair Lighting. While many photographers make hair lighting a part of their everyday portrait setup, Rolando prefers to reserve this look for when separation is required or when he wants to accent the highlights in blond hair. "If I just want a clean beauty shot and the beauty is the face of the subject, I normally don't accent the hair with a hair light," he says. "The reason is simple: the eyes will always go to the lightest part of the image, and hair lights tend to highlight the hair, not the face. If the purpose of my shot is to show the model's facial beauty, using a hair light is contradictory to my goals—especially in a tightly cropped image where part of the hair is cropped out."

Accent Lighting. Accent (or "edge") lights are commonly used in "Playboy style" glamour photography. Rolando recalls a spec shoot he once did for a submission to Playboy Special Editions where he used *nine* lights. This included a main light directed right into the model's face, a kicker light bouncing into a California Sunbounce reflector (placed on the floor and aimed back at the model to fill underneath

This setup shot of *Playboy* Playmate Holley (above) illustrates the use of two Hensel Beauty Dishes. The main dish has the typical center reflector dome and no grid. The second was placed low and pointed toward the background. This dish has the center dome and no grid, so the 22-inch dish provides a wide spread of light to evenly illuminate the background and bring out the color of the flame-red seamless paper. The shot at the top is the result of this lighting setup. (CAMERA: Olympus E-1)

Here, both Hensel Beauty Dishes had the center reflector removed and replaced with grids. The main dish had a 10-degree grid while the background dish had a 20-degree grid in the center. Notice Holley's pupils in both images. The image with the dome removed and the more direct grid light makes the pupils smaller and creates a more feathered look for both the background and the light on the model. The intensity of the light increased here by at least one f/stop. (CAMERA: Olympus E-1)

her face), one hair light, two background lights to simulate sun coming through windows, and four accent lights. The accent lights highlighted the edges of several parts of the model's body, which varied depending on the pose. One light skimmed across the model's buttocks when she was laying down, another would strike the edge of her shoulders when she was sitting up. Yet another hit the other side of her shoulders, while a fourth light skimmed across the model's calves. "This type of setup—often with even more lights—is what Playboy prefers; it's their style of lighting," says Rolando.

Great accent lighting doesn't have to involve nearly a dozen studio lights, though. Rolando finds plenty of ways to create it on location simply by being aware of his environment and keeping his eyes open for lighting opportunities. "When working on location, I like to walk the site—especially if it is a private residence," he says. "Sometimes I'll stumble into a master bath that has glass-block windows with beautiful natural light filtering in. That type of light can be used as a main, edge, or even hair light. You can also get beautiful edge lighting by going outside and placing your subject underneath a tree with her back at the line where shade and light meet."

Warming Gels. Rolando often uses warming gels on his accent lights or main light. One he recommends is the Rosco #02, known in cinema photography as a "Bastard Amber." This gives the model some color, similar to the warming effect of the setting sun. "These give your subject a little more personality," he says.

Kristen was photographed with a Larson 48-inch Soff Strip with a Lighttools 40-degree grid and a Rosco #3410 1/8 CTO warming gel. The model was posed with her shoulders slightly turned to accent her bustline. Here, the hat acts as a prop to further set the mood and to shape her face. (CAMERA: Olympus E-1)

SHADOWS

Often, photographers concentrate on lighting an image; Rolando prefers to concentrate, instead, on creating the shadows. He suggests that an easy way to practice looking for shadows and how they appear on your subject is to have your model step back away from the light into the darkness. As your subject walks slowly forward into the light, pay close attention to where the shadows fall. Stop her along the

Trixie was lit by a Larson 48-inch Soff Strip with a 40-degree Lighttools honeycomb grid. The grid mounted on the front of the box added a slight increase in contrast while focusing the light away from the black seamless background. Notice how the shadow areas separate her chin from her neck and shape her cleavage. (CAMERA: Olympus E-1)

way and have her turn her body. Experiment with having her turn only her upper body, only her lower body, only her head, and then her entire body. Do this in increments as she walks toward the light and closely observe the effects produced.

Keep in mind that changes in the subject's pose will change how shadows are formed on her face and body. "For example," says Rolando, "if my subject is laying on her side and she pulls her upper leg down in front of the lower leg, the body tends to appear thicker at the thighs. To compensate for this, I position my lights to create a shadow down the side of the thigh, in essence cutting about a third of the thigh out of the light. As you can imagine, this leads to a more flattering and slimming position."

If the model's hand is posed frontally and toward the camera (like when arms cross in the front of the subject and the hands fall on the upper arms), Rolando tries to create a slight shadow on the hands. "This reduces the impact of the entire hand," he notes, "keeping the viewer's eyes on the face."

Shadow can also be used to correct problems or accent assets. A small shadow under the chin, for example, creates separation from the neck. This is very important if your subject tends to have a double chin. On the other hand, turning your subject's body slightly away from the light slims her figure and creates a shadow on the cleavage area, making it look fuller.

"If you haven't guessed it already," says Rolando, "I love shadows."

IN CLOSING

For Rolando, glamour lighting involves technical prowess but also an intuitive sense of what makes your subject look her best. Therefore, he recommends you work slowly and make it your practice to carefully observe the effects of changing the subject and light positions as you create each shot. "Stick to single-light setups until you feel you've mastered them, then move on to two-light setups, and so on," he says. "It's up to you to decide if the effect a style of lighting produces is suited to your subject, your style of photography, and the image you're creating."

5. MICHAEL BIONDO

Simple Beauty in a Complicated World

For portrait photographers, creating a salable product usually involves pleasing just two people: the photographer and the subject. The preparation might involve consulting with the client, then setting up the backdrop, lights, etc.

For acclaimed fashion photographer Michael Biondo, however, getting things just right might involve a month or more of planning, numerous meetings to discuss the intended "feel" of the images, and even building and painting custom backdrops for the shoot. Sound complicated? Well, things are really just getting started.

On the day of a major shoot, it's not uncommon for Michael to have as many as twenty or thirty people on the set—from hair, fashion, and makeup stylists, to models, client reps, and assistants for everyone (Michael often brings two or three of his own). For this reason, Michael says that fashion photographers have to be as much directors as photographers. "A major fashion shoot and advertising campaign is a high-stakes game and there is a lot of money involved," says Biondo. "The person who hired me has his or her job on the line—in fact, for the duration of the shoot, whether it's a day or a week, they have put their career in my hands."

With so much on the line and so many creative people involved in each shoot, it may be surprising that the word Michael uses most often when describing the look he wants in his lighting is "simple." In fact, when it comes to lighting, Michael often chooses to use a single source—and the results he achieves with it are nothing short of breathtaking. So if you think beautifully crafted, artistic lighting has to be complicated, think again. As you'll see in the images discussed in this chapter, a master of photographic lighting can produce truly superb results—indoors or out—with the simplest of setups.

DIRECTIONAL, DIFFUSED LIGHTING

The first time Biondo took a digital camera on location, he shot the image seen in the next spread (and on the cover of this book). He created it as a test

MICHAEL BIONDO is a New York based photographer who has enjoyed a successful career in editorial and advertising photography for the past eighteen years. After graduating from Pratt Institute with a degree in fine art, Michael began photographing celebrities. He shot for *Interview, Rolling Stone, Entertainment Weekly, Vogue,* and Sony Music. In 1993, Michael moved to Paris to specialize in fashion photography. There, his clients included Giorgio Armani, Emanuel Ungaro, Valentino, and *W* magazine. In the mid-1990s, Michael returned to New York, where he has since shot for *Harper's Bazaar, Glamour, Elle,* Saks Fifth Avenue, Neiman Marcus, and Virgin Records. He has photographed numerous celebrities, including Janet Jackson, Beyoncé, Ed Harris, and James Earl Jones. For more on Michael Biondo, please visit www.MichaelBiondo.com.

while he was waiting for the Polaroids to come up. He showed it to the client and she was so blown away that she immediately used it in an advertisement—a two-page spread in *InStyle* magazine. "And this is a client who is very particular about detail," notes Biondo, "because these dresses are all about detail."

The image was shot in a castle where there was a bank of windows to camera right. Biondo shot Dyna-Lite strobes with standard reflectors through the windows to mimic the look of sunlight; outside it actually was pitch black and pouring rain.

"I hung some diffusion over the windows," says Biondo, "but I could not have the strobes out in the rain. So to keep them from blowing up, we covered them with white kitchen garbage bags."

"To this day, we joke that what made this light so fantastic was the garbage bags. The light was diffused by the bag, then the 12x12-foot diffuser on the window, and then the dirty glass. By the time it hit the model, it was this beautiful light—but it had direction because the original source was a high-contrast light."

FEEL IT OUT

Both of the images shown to the left were shot for Saks Fifth Avenue, and both were created using a single light source: a small Chimera strip light with one Profoto head and one Profoto power pack. In each case, the light was placed high up and angled down toward the model. "One light is really all you need," says Biondo. "You can move really quickly with a setup like this. With the light on a boom, you can move it around and try to be as intuitive as possible without letting all the equipment and technology get in the way. The placement is really by feel; you see how the light falls on the subject and on the set."

CRANK THE ISO

The photograph on the facing page was shot in a barn with one Kino Flo (a fluorescent source). "I really love Kino Flos," says Biondo, "but they don't put out a lot of light. If you're able to crank the ISO, however—as you can with the Canon 1ds Mark II—you can use them." The only other light used in this image was a strobe, which was fired through a window off to the model's right to brighten the background. This image was created for *Elle* magazine.

A HALLWAY OF LIGHT

The image above was shot using a bank of windows to camera right as the main source of light. To camera left, Biondo hung two 12x12-foot white griflons, bouncing light back onto the model and creating what amounted to a hallway. "She basically just walked back and forth in this hallway we constructed," says Biondo.

BRINGING THE OUTDOORS INSIDE

Biondo is know for shooting outdoor images with a studio-lit quality. In the image to the right, he used rear projection to accomplish the reverse—bringing the outdoors into the studio. "Studio-style images created outdoors always look a little surreal," says

Biondo, "so I wanted the same look here."

The key light on the subject was a small Kino Flo light placed to camera right "I'm very into simple lighting—one or two lights maximum. I get bogged down if there's too much stuff and too many choices to make," says Biondo. Keeping it simple allows him to respond fluidly to each situation and make the most of each opportunity.

A BREAK IN THE TREES

The top image on this page was created using natural light—except for the light hitting her back, which came from a small Chimera with a 30-degree fabric grid. This light was placed just off camera but close to the model and aimed down so it did not hit her face. The pool was surrounded by trees, but there was a break to the right just beyond the pool. The light through this clearing lit the pool and produced the highlight on her cheek and the side of her body. The photo was created for Australian *Harper's Bazaar*.

ADD A REFLECTOR

This image (bottom left) was created in Cabo san Lucas on the same trip as the image seen on page 54. Biondo shot the image in a hotel courtyard with midday sun crashing down on the model from above. "When this happens," says Biondo, "you just have to find a situation that works. Then, if you position the fill properly, you can open up the

shadows by two or three stops." Here, he did just that, using a white reflector to camera right.

MAKING THE MOST OF IT

The image above was produced for Saks Fifth Avenue. The shot was created on a rooftop with the city skyline in the background. The tricky part of the photo? Just like the previous image, it was created in the middle of the day with harsh sunlight beating down on the scene from directly overhead.

"That was not by *my* choice," notes Biondo. "As a commercial photographer, so much is just a response to the situation you're placed in—the model is only available at this time, the client needs the image right away, etc. You learn to deal with it."

In this case, the light was so harsh that Biondo had to totally overpower it to dump the background. He chose a medium strip Chimera as the key. The result is a dramatically lit shot that looks more like a twilight image than one taken at midday.

LIGHTING WITH PHOTOSHOP

The image on the next page was shot in Cabo san Lucas for *Elle* magazine. Biondo used only natural

light from a partially overcast sky, but he pumped the light up a bit in Photoshop.

"Using Photoshop as a digital darkroom is great. Effects you'd need a truckload of equipment to create in camera, you can now do in postproduction," says Biondo. "It's the same vision, except it wouldn't have been possible to make this photograph without Photoshop. I was on one rock and she was on another rock, but both of those rocks were about 40 feet in the air on a remote island beach." Even if it would have been feasible to bring in the equipment to create this shot, it would have taken all day to make the photo. "The client would never have approved spending that long on a single image," says Biondo, "so without Photoshop, the image simply would not have been made.

While on location, each shot was downloaded to a 17-inch laptop so the art director could watch the progress. Back at the hotel, Biondo brightened the model up a little, darkened the background, and

added a little contrast—things he *could* have done with light on location, but which were infinitely easier to accomplish in postproduction.

USING "FOUND" REFLECTORS

The image above (right) was also shot for *Elle* magazine using natural light. Biondo shot it in an area of Brooklyn where there are lots of old warehouses. There was a building behind him with a light gray stucco facade. As you can see from the highlights on the model's hair and face, bright sun was streaming in from camera left. However, the light bouncing off the stucco building provided so much fill that she was still beautifully lit. "When I started using objects around me as reflectors," says Biondo, "it really changed the way I looked at lighting."

With setups like this, Michael Biondo's elegant work proves that complexity is not a prerequisite for success when it comes to lighting. In fact, the simple beauty of a single source can be incredibly effective.

6. JEFFREY AND JULIA WOODS

Shedding Light on Everyday Life

For Jeffrey and Julia Woods, who operate a successful wedding and portrait studio, successful photography is all about real life. While many photographers strive to create a fantasy, Jeff and Julia look for ways to capture images that are meaningful to their clients because they reflect the places, activities, and relationships they love.

Creating such work relies on the the couple's ability to establish a strong personal relationship with each client, relationships they regard so highly that they have trouble referring to many of their past subjects as "clients"—they're more like friends. "We won't

do any session without a consultation," says Jeff. "Sometimes there are reasons we have to do it on the phone (like the client lives out of town), but getting to know the client is critical to our shoot."

As the images in this chapter show, this strategy helps them produce images that are both creative and highly marketable.

NECESSITY BREEDS INVENTION

A scheduling mix-up due to daylight-savings time meant shooting this image (left) well after sunset. However, necessity bred invention and Jeff and Julia discovered a technique they now use regularly. Shooting with a video light aimed through a scrim, the camera's white balance was set to tungsten. This rendered the skin tones warm but, because of the rapid falloff of the source, produced a dramatic blue cast on the background.

BUILT-IN SHOOTING AREAS

Jeff and Julia's studio is designed to incorporate shooting areas. The shot on the facing page was created in their production room against a roughed-up

JEFFREY AND JULIA WOODS operate a successful wedding and portrait studio that specializes in highly personalized images that reflect the tastes and experiences that make each client unique. Their elegant images have been featured in *Rangefinder* magazine and in numerous photography books. In addition, their acclaimed marketing strategies have become the basis for a successful educational program for professional photographers, which they run out of their studio in Washington, IL. To learn more, visit www.jwportraitlife.com or www.jwweddinglife.com.

plaster wall. The subject was seated on a stool and illuminated by a Westcott Spiderlight, a portable soft box that houses five fluorescent lights.

CATALOGING LOCATIONS

The top-left image on the facing page, a portrait of the couple's daughter, was taken on the spur of the moment when they happened upon an area with great light. They are always looking for new shooting spots for location sessions—especially ones where they don't have to mess with the light. This allows them to use the freer shooting style they prefer. In this case, they have found that the location, in the corner of a building, has great light from midday on. They later used the same location to create the image seen on page 64.

HIGH-KEY LIGHT

While they tend to prefer continuous sources, in their high-key shooting area Jeff and Julia rely on strobe. For the shot at the bottom of the facing page they used two soft boxes to create consistent light across the shooting area. This meant they didn't have to worry about keeping their subject in one spot.

In this case, Julia had to run the shoot because the little girl wanted nothing to do with Jeff. Once she got the girl laughing and making goofy faces by making some gentle jokes about her dad, however, Julia was able to capture a series of images with great natural expressions.

NATURAL MOMENTS

In the two images above, late-day natural light was the sole source of illumination. The image on the left features an elegant chair that provides a great place for posing the girls as well as an unexpected element in an outdoor shot. For a bigger group, they might use a couch for the same feel (see page 61).

The image on the right is actually a candid shot taken at a wedding as the little girl wandered around in a field at the bride's parents' home. Facing into the setting sun, she was bathed in golden light.

SHOOTING AT DUSK

If the pre-session consultation reveals that the clients love golfing or have a favorite pet, you can bet that Jeff and Julia will find a way to incorporate that knowledge into their portraits. The consultation also gives them some insight on the types of products the client will likely be purchasing. This allows them to sculpt the session that will best suit the clients' needs and tastes. If they know it will be a big sale, they insist on doing the outdoor portraits at dusk. "If they're going to make an investment in us," says Jeff, "we owe it to them to set up a shoot that we know will provide the best results."

For the portrait seen below, the family was photographed at dusk in open shade. Autumn foliage provides the perfect complementary background for their matching blue jeans. But where are the faces? "We were *trying* to get the dog to stand up," laughs Julia, "but he just wouldn't. In the end, we gave in to what *he* wanted." It's an unusual shot, but the family liked it so much they bought a wall-size portrait. It also hangs in Jeff and Julia's studio, where it always attracts attention. And why not? It tells a great story about this fun, relaxed family.

Two other late-day portraits are seen on the facing page. For the family portrait at the top, Jeff and Julia prepared the setup and then waited for the area to fall into shade as the sun dropped. Shooting down at an angle eliminated any potential hot spots in the background.

For the engagement portrait seen at the bottom of the page, the sun from behind the couple provided beautiful rim lighting that highlights the loving look on the future groom's face. Getting the couple into their element and keeping the shoot simple helped produce these natural expressions.

KEEP IT SIMPLE

Even when they shoot in the studio, Jeff and Julia are always looking for ways to produce light that doesn't look like it was created in the studio. In the image to the left (top), they used a single soft box with a continuous light source as the main light and a nearby white wall for fill. The result is clean, simple light that lets the little girl's intense expression steal the show.

MIDDAY LIGHT

While evening light is best, sometimes it's necessary to shoot at midday. In the portrait to the left (bottom), Jeff and Julia photographed this senior in a situation with plenty of blockers. They just added a reflector to light her face. The result is a dramatic backlit portrait. "My favorite part is the burst of lens flare at the top," says Jeff.

A LITTLE RESEARCH, A LITTLE PATIENCE

An image like the one on the facing page requires a great consultation. In this case, the couple found out that their client absolutely loved playing polo. To create the perfect shot for him, they waited until late in the day when about half of the polo field dropped into shade. Then, they set themselves up to get backlighting on the subject and his horse. Once they had the right setup, Jeff and Julia told the subject to stay in the shade and had him ride back and forth, making a pass through the area of good lighting. It took some patience to get everything just right, but the results are worth it. Jeff says, "Look at his expression and his pose. I didn't have to coach him because it was all natural—he loves polo." And that's where their research really pays off.

TWO LOOKS, ONE CLIENT

The images on the facing page and above (left) were both created with one client. The styling, clothing selection, and lighting, however, give them two distinctive looks. The image on the facing page, shot in the corner of a building, has earthy tones throughout the frame. The feel is polished but still very laid back—a quality enhanced by light digital softening.

In the image above, the high-school senior's look is much more dramatic. In addition to a clothing change, Jeff and Julia moved the subject to an area where a lucite wall, lit from within, served as the backdrop. A window in front of her provided the main light while a reflector and the light bouncing off the room's white marble floor added ample fill.

BOOSTING THE DRAMA

One of the Woods' favorite shooting areas is a nearby field with a barn and abandoned house. The portrait above (right) was taken at midday with the subject standing inside the house near two windows with no glass in them. The result is great side-lighting.

While the shot was already dramatic, Jeff enhanced the drama in postproduction. This is something that he considers a big part of what separates professional photographers from photo enthusiasts. "In the art production phase," he says, "we can create more mood than in the straight photo."

The couple has two highly-trained graphic designers on staff to assist in the process. As a result, clients never see an image that is not completely finished to the studio's specifications. "This makes it much easier to sell," says Julia. "Clients see a great photo and get connected to it immediately. Then they *can't* leave without buying it."

Julia is quick to note, however, that their objective is to gently enhance the client's appearance, never to change it so much that it looks unnatural.

TWO LOOKS, ONE SETTING

Jeff and Julia's studio is located in a small, historic town, and they take full advantage of the aesthetic opportunities that affords them.

One great feature of the town is that it has a few cobblestone brick streets, which make great backdrops for portraits—especially when shooting down from a high angle. This allows the bricks to fill up the entire background, as seen in these two shots.

Yet, despite the fact that both shots employ the same setting, the light used to create them and the postproduction processing makes the two images vastly different in their character.

In the first image (above), the couple wanted to create a "tough guy" look for their subject. The sun was close to setting when they began working on the shot, so the houses on either side of the street created a shaft of light that illuminated the young man from behind. It's much harsher lighting than they would usually use for a portrait, but it was perfect for accenting his physique with rim light and creating the rough look they wanted for the shot.

Complementing this look in the final image are the cool and subdued colors on the bricks, which are almost blue. It's a portrait that's all "guy."

On the facing page, the street served as a nonseasonal backdrop for a winter engagement portrait. "In our climate, there's no foliage during the winter," notes Jeff. "It's not very pretty, so we have to look for other options if we want to continue to do outdoor portraits.

The day they chose to create this portrait actually turned out to be overcast, so the light was very soft. "The sky was like a big natural soft box," says Jeff. As

a result, the light on the subjects is extremely soft. Yet, notice the delicate highlights it still creates on her face.

What really makes the image communicate the right message about the couple is the rosy tones used throughout the frame (compare the bricks here with those in the image above) and the couple's naturally romantic pose. Both lend the photograph a sunny warmth that makes the viewer think more about how much in love they are than about how cold they might be in their winter garb.

IN HIS ELEMENT

Here's another pair of images that show how hard the couple works to create images that capture the subject in his element.

In this case, the young man was a skateboarder, so they found an urban-looking location where they could capture him in action. Working in open shade, they just let him do his thing and captured action shots as he zoomed through the frame (below).

As seen on the facing page, they also captured a much different portrait of the young man. This image was created in open shade in an outside area with an overhang. A reflector was used for fill.

CONCLUSION

When Jeff and Julia approach a portrait session, their goal is to capture something real—something that reflects the way the subjects actually live. As a result, the lighting effects they choose are deliberately uncomplicated and natural looking.

When shooting in the studio, the use of continuous sources softened through scrims helps make the shooting process more natural and fluid, since they can always see exactly what they're getting. Outdoors, getting great natural-light images means selecting the right locations and working in them at the right time of day. Jeff and Julia strive to find locations where the light is so good they can use it as is, or maybe with just a bit of fill.

This strategy lets the couple really concentrate on their subjects instead of fiddling with unnecessarily complex lighting setups. As a result, they can spend the time they need to put the clients at ease and break down the walls that sometimes prevent photographers from getting the best-possible images with each subject. It's the final step in a process that began with the consultation.

This highly personalized approach yields images that are inherently meaningful to the clients—images that virtually sell themselves.

HCO
WELCOME
TO Fabulous
LAS VEGAS
NEVADA

7. KEVIN FOLEY

Lighting with Character

When he steps behind the camera, Kevin Foley has an important objective: to make his subject look good. While that might seem obvious (not to mention incredibly modest), Foley points out that it's not every photographer's goal. After all, it's easy to get caught up in your creative impulses and start designing images that are interesting for your portfolio . . . but maybe not exactly flattering.

As Foley's engaging images show, however, it's not an either/or situation. Flattering the subject doesn't mean avoiding the creative risks that can result in great portfolio images—it means finding a balance. This is something that Foley does with grace, crafting images that catch your eye with their creativity but capture it with their beauty.

DELICATE HIGHLIGHTS

The images to the right and on the facing page were shot several years ago for Kodak to demonstrate the capabilities of a new digital camera. One of Foley's objectives in designing the images was to produce highlights that showed off the camera's ability to hold detail in these very bright areas—something that could be a struggle with many early digitals.

KEVIN FOLEY is a fashion and celebrity photographer based in Los Angeles. He has shot for numerous television and film campaigns, in addition to extensive editorial and catalog assignments. Among the famous faces he has photographed are Jay Leno, Brooke Shields, Matt LeBlanc, Rob Lowe, Debra Messing, and Morgan Freeman. His clients include NBC, BET Television, ABC, Paramount Pictures, Warner Brothers, Showtime, and *Razor Magazine*. To learn more about Foley's work and view additional images, please visit www.foleyphoto.com.

For the first image (page 70), Foley used white V-flats on either side of the model. Each flat was fitted with two strobe heads. These were placed at about waist and shoulder height. This lighting setup created the long, bright highlights that run the length of the model's body. A 5-foot Elinchrom Octabank soft box was then placed over the camera to fill in from the front.

For the second image (previous page), the Elinchrom soft box was moved to the side of the model and a white board was moved in on the left.

SIMPLE BEAUTY

Like most photographers, Foley is a fan of natural light and looks for locations where he only needs to refine it to get the results he wants. "I like to use the

major features of what's already there," he says. "I try to find beautiful light, then fill in where the natural light isn't working, so it looks perfect." For many of his shoots, this requires some scouting—and some imagination to determine the best time of day for shooting at any given location.

The images below and on the facing page were shot with the model reclining on a couch. For both

images, the main light source was window light from 6x8-foot diffused panes to camera left. (The top-left image on page 74 was shot in the same location and shows the windows used.)

For the horizontal shot (left), a reflector was added below and to the right of the model to provide fill (note the tiny secondary catchlight in her eyes). Foley got down to the model's eye level to compose this image.

Less fill was used on the vertical image (above), producing light that is still soft but with a slightly

higher ratio. Foley shot this image from above with the model looking up at the camera and her arms raised to frame her face. Note the triangle of light on her left cheek, characteristic of the classic Rembrandt portrait lighting pattern.

STRIKING A BALANCE

To create light that was in harmony with the large window in the background of this shot (above left), Foley placed an Elinchrom Octabank soft box to camera left and used a white board to the right for reflected fill. An umbrella was used to camera left behind the model to fill in the 30 to 40 feet of open space between her and the window.

For the above-right image, Foley used two medium soft boxes behind the model, both fitted with warming gels. A white board was used for fill, and a 5-foot Elinchrom Octabank was placed directly behind the camera, which was situated in a doorway.

Like the images on the previous two pages, the photos above were created for a clothing catalog. Notice how Foley sculpted the light to display the colors and textures of the fabrics—but without compromising on the appeal of the lighting on the models' faces.

DRAMA

Foley tends to prefer soft light, but for the photo on the facing page he wanted a more dramatic look. This image was created after a catalog shoot when the makeup artist, who was taken with the model's look, asked if Foley wanted to stick around and do

some additional images. The makeup artist created this bold look, and Foley photographed the model in a nearby freight elevator using a Beauty Dish almost straight over her head.

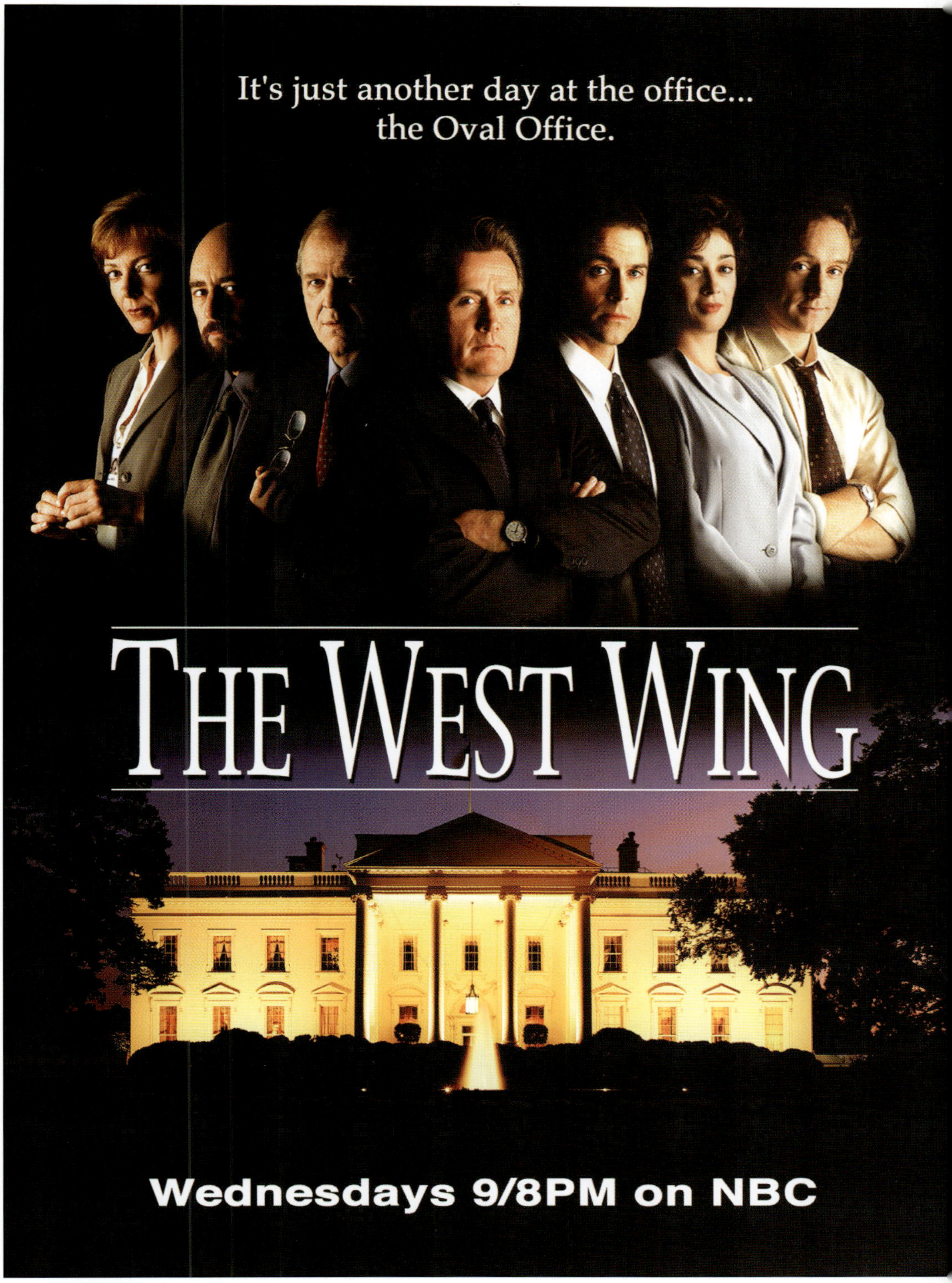

STRENGTH

For many of his shoots, Foley photographs actors who need to be shown in character—or at least in a way that suits the character they play in the program or film that is being promoted. In this case (facing page), Rob Lowe was photographed for *The West Wing*.

The concept of the shoot was to have one side of the subject in highlight and the other side in shadow. The look was designed to suggest the power and intrigue of national politics.

While the concept may have been quite weighty, the execution of the portrait shows that simple lighting can often be extremely effective. Foley created this shot by posing his subject in front of a black backdrop. He then used a single Chimera soft box to camera right as the main light.

To further increase the lighting ratio, a black card was used as a gobo to camera left, reducing spill on the shadow side of the face and allowing it to drop into deep shadow. Had this image (actually an outtake from the session) been selected for the final shot, Foley notes that the area around the subject's ear would probably have been burned in to eliminate any detail on that side of the face.

Each of the lead actors on the program were photographed in the same way. Later, the images were combined to create the cast photo that was used in advertising for the series (above). Why go to the trouble of compositing the images when all the actors were available on the same set? Well, take another look at the image. The effect defies physics.

If the actors had been photographed as a single group, the main light on the subjects to the right would have spilled onto the shadow areas of the subjects on the left (and vice versa). Digital compositing was what made this image possible.

SERIOUSLY TROPICAL

So what do you do when your location and the mood you need to create are inherently at odds? That's what happened in the image of Eric Balfour seen on the facing page. The shot was created to promote a television series set in Hawaii (thus the location), but it was a *drama*—something a sunny beach doesn't suggest. To lend the image a more serious air, Foley significantly overpowered the sunlight using an Elinchrom Octabank soft box to camera right (this is what creates the highlight on the actor's jaw). An umbrella was also used to camera right and was balanced by a white board for fill to camera left. Notice that the supplemental light sources are in harmony with the existing light. Adding them simply allowed the cheerful background to be rendered in more subdued tones, appropriate to the flavor of the show.

MALE SUBJECTS

As you can see in the images shown here (and the image of Rob Lowe on page 76), male subjects are often lit as much for character as attractiveness.

Foley photographed Jesse Metcalfe (above right) for a *Razor Magazine* feature on hot young Hollywood stars. For a look that rendered the actor as handsome but also a little edgy, Foley used a Beauty Dish above and to the left of the subject. To the right, an umbrella was bounced into a white board for diffused fill. Behind the subject, two umbrellas skimmed across the background for an even tonality.

Morgan Freeman (right) was photographed for a story on his production company. The near symmetry of the pose and low key of the image send just the right message for this purpose. Foley actually created the shoot on the roof of the building where Freeman's office is located. He erected a black backdrop and placed a large soft box above and slightly to the left of the subject. Since a dark background like this

THE
Tonight
SHOW
WITH
JAY LENO

can overemphasize facial contours, Foley added a white board below the subject to open up the shadows. Combined with the light from an overcast day, the result is both flattering and very natural looking.

AN INSIDE LOOK

Foley happened to be in Washington, D.C., speaking for Kodak when he received a call to photograph Jay Leno. Because Leno does so much political humor, he came up with the idea of a blue-screen image showing him with some iconic buildings. Foley shot the buildings before leaving Washington, then created digital composites after he photographed Leno. His favorite part of this image? The inside of the dome, which is (of course) entirely fabricated.

WINTER WONDERLAND?

Foley created the two images to the right for a *Razor Magazine* feature on winter fashions. Due to the production schedule, however, the shoot was in June. The solution was to use fake snow—and it's pretty convincing. "If there's a giveaway," Foley laughs, "it's the green foliage in the first shot [top]."

To get just the right look in the action image (snow flying, hair tossing), Foley shot between fifty and a hundred frames. Fortunately, having the instant feedback digital affords let him know right away what was working. The light was supplied by a 5-foot Elinchrom Octabank soft box to camera right (behind the dog). Two white boards were also used: one to the left of the female model and one to camera right, slightly behind the camera position.

For the second image (bottom), Foley posed the models on a porch with an opening to camera left that served as the main light. Fill was supplied by a white board below the models and to camera right.

CONCLUSION

Kevin Foley's images show how important light can be to the character of an image. From vibrant fashion shots to moody character studies, light is a critical means of communication in photography. And when it's also used to make every subject look their very best, so much the better!

8. CORDETTA SPELLS

Natural Light Brings Life to Her Images

When Cordetta Spells named her business "Life's Images," she wasn't messing around. In her years behind the camera, both as a television news videographer and now as a still photographer, she has seen life from all sides—sorrows and joys, triumphs and tragedies. Working on the front line of these events as a photojournalist, however, she wasn't just an observer; she experienced each moment right alongside the key players. Today, when she photographs weddings, portraits, or commercial work, she still puts herself in the middle of the action and draws on her photojournalism skills to produce images that are uniquely imbued with life.

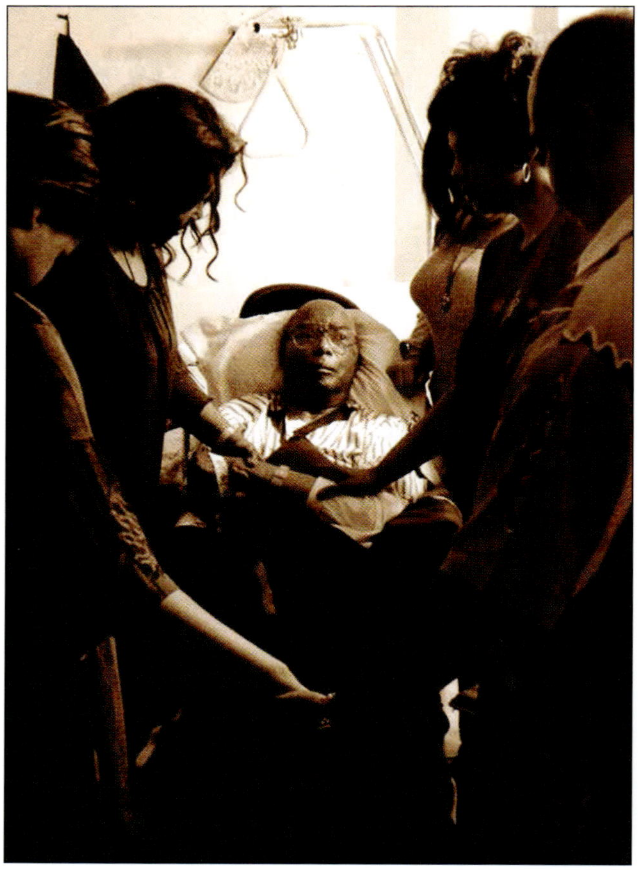

When it comes to lighting, she enjoys using existing light whenever possible. In part, this is due to experience; when shooting news stories, her choices were limited to either harsh video lighting or natural light, which is almost always more appealing. A second motivation is the sheer challenge of using natural light to create portraits. "There's nothing wrong with using studio lighting—you can do anything with it," says Cordetta. "I just like to see how much

CORDETTA SPELLS was interested in photography from a young age, and when it came time to go to college, she decided to major in broadcast journalism. "I learned to shoot and shot for about twenty years," she says. During that time, she documented famous faces (from Bill Clinton to Rosa Parks), professional sports, local and national news events, and much more. She also won two Emmys and numerous other awards, working as one of only six female African American field photographers in the country at the time. When she went on disability from her job behind the video camera, she decided to step behind a still camera and open up a photography business. Today, she owns and operates Life's Images, where she does wedding, portrait, and commerial photography. To see more of Cordetta's images, visit www.lifesimages-photography.com

I can do with the raw materials that exist in a scene." Whether it's in a dining room or on the beach, Cordetta has found great ways to do just that—as the images in this chapter show.

THANKSGIVING

This photograph of Cordetta's ailing father (facing page) was taken at home on Thanksgiving as his loving family stood around him saying grace. Something told her it might be his last Thanksgiving, so she grabbed her camera and took one shot. As it happened, he passed away a week before the next Thanksgiving. "People see that picture and cry," she says.

BEACHWALK

The subject of the photos on this page gave birth about three days after the shoot. When the mom-to-be scheduled the session, she was open to suggestions. Cordetta thought a beach shot would be nice, and scheduled the session at sunset to take advantage of a beautifully colored sky and the low angle of the light to backlight her subject. After the shoot, the tones of the sunset in the background were enhanced, and the woman's figure was rendered as more of a silhouette (bottom photo), since the detail on her form wasn't as important as the shape of her round belly. Cordetta also experimented with using a warming filter during this shoot (top photo) to enhance the golden tones in the scene.

MARY

When a visitor to a photo expo saw Cordetta's image of her father (facing page), she shared the story of her own mother, who was a cancer patient.

Cordetta suggested they take some pictures while the mother was still alive. A few weeks later, the daughter called. Although Cordetta arrived soon after the family received bad news about Mary's condition, she spent some time with the mother and daughter and eventually made them laugh. Before long, Mary was up and about, dancing and playing piano with her daughter. "She was talking about what hot stuff she was back in school," laughs Cordetta.

Mary wanted a picture taken with her hair being combed, but as it turned out, only a few strands were holding her hair on. "I told her, 'If it was up to me and I was trying to fight cancer, I'd shave my head before I'd let cancer take my hair,'" says Cordetta. The first photo in the series (above, left) was then taken with Mary getting her newly shaved scalp washed. Cordetta leaned down into the sink and used only available light for the image. She then vignetted the shot to keep viewers' focus on Mary's emotional face.

About four weeks later, Cordetta created the second image, called *Letting Go* (top right). It was taken when they knew that Mary was passing. She shot it with the fluourescent lights in Mary's hospital room.

The final image is called *First Goodbye* (bottom right). "I loved the fact that the older grandson was stoic, but the younger one just couldn't take it," says Cordetta. Notice the subtlety of the image; the two boys' reactions tell you the whole story. Cordetta created the image in the church where Mary's funeral was held, using the bright light from a high window to add a heavenly quality to the story.

MOOD

Often, the mood she wants to convey dictates the lighting Cordetta looks for. With kids, it's most often light and airy—but not always. As the images on the facing page show, more subdued looks can also be effective. In the flower girl image (top left) and mother–daughter portrait (bottom right), the darker tones help convey a more serious mood. The young man seen in the top-right image was photographed at a wedding just a couple of years ago, but it has the look of an image taken in an old Southern Methodist church—a sense the darker tones reinforce. Cordetta created the bottom-left photo as a headshot and

TELL THE STORY

When making the transition from videography to still photography, Cordetta was conscious to keep storytelling a powerful part of her images. "If you can watch a television news story with the sound down and still tell what happening, someone's done a great job of storytelling," she says. "That's how I still work, but I don't have the time to let different shots tell the story. I just have one frame to get it right."

The images on this and the facing page were all created as promotional images for musicians, so she wanted to communicate that sensibility in each shot. In addition, she wanted the viewer to know instantly what kind of music each artist played.

For the shots above, created for a gospel performer, she selected an outdoor location for a bright and airy tone. The intense light from above cast a

photographed it in color. Converting the image to black & white and darkening the tones in Photoshop totally transformed the shot, emphasizing the symmetry of his face and the intensity of his eyes. "It made the difference between a photo that makes people say, 'What a cute boy' and one that makes fine-art buyers say, 'I'll pay you $1200 for that,'" says Cordetta.

heavenly glow on the subject, a characteristic that was emphasized by the use of a low camera angle (top) and backlighting with lens flare (bottom).

For the images below, created for a jazz musician, Cordetta wanted to create a mood that was more smoky and intense—as though the subject was in a jazz club. Using contrasty lighting through her dining room window, Cordetta worked with the subject on a series of images that have just the right flavor. She joked with the subject to get him to smile, bringing out the lines on his face to add dimension and texture to the image.

ROSARY

This bride wanted to make sure her wedding images included a photograph of her grandmother's rosary. Rather than just grab a standard shot, Cordetta watched the light and positioned the bride so the rosary created a shadow on her gown (below). She then framed the image tightly to capture some details of the dress and gloves but keep the focus of the image on the rosary.

The rosary image was created in the same spot as the portrait to the left of the bride being attended to by her four bridesmaids. Both images were actually created within a few minutes of each other as Cordetta explored the room and looked for ways to take advantage of all the possibilities the window light had to offer.

The pair of images, so different in their character, shows how versatile natural light can be when it is used by someone with a practiced eye and good creative instincts. These are just the skills that Cordetta perfected in her years as a photojournalist—and her clients now enjoy the beautiful results.

9. CHRISTOPHER GREY

Light—The Greatest Tool of All

Digital technology has changed many aspects of professional photography. From the ability to instantly preview images to the increased responsibilities of building and maintaining a color-managed workflow, digital has truly been a revolution. Yet, despite the many changes, the key elements that go into making a creative and successful image have remained the same. "No matter how archaic or contemporary the process you use to create a portrait, knowledge of composition, technical expertise, familiarity with your equipment, and a high degree of competence and confidence are all tools that contribute to your creativity," says Minneapolis, MN, photographer Christopher Grey.

While photographers have the ability to fine-tune an almost limitless number of variables in each image they produce, Grey feels strongly that light is the greatest tool of all. "To my mind," he says, "light is a living thing, vibrant and malleable. As a professional photographer, I know I can create a more impressive and interesting portrait in any situation where I can control the light—and make no mistake, *control* is the operative word. Some say it's a poor carpenter who blames his tools. I'll never blame light for what it does, but I love it for what it can do."

What light does for Grey is pretty remarkable. In this chapter, he shares some of his favorite techniques for using this most powerful of tools.

WORKING WITH FALLOFF

Light weakens as it travels away from its source. The inverse square law is the equation used to calculate this light falloff. It states that light intensity is inversely proportional to the square of the distance from the light to the subject. In more practical terms, it means that if you double the distance between the source and the subject, the light reaching the subject will be only a quarter as strong, because it has twice as far to travel. "While this is a law of physics and therefore absolute, it is *visually* absolute only when dealing with one light source in a dark room," notes Grey. "Many other factors, such as ambient light in the room or spill from other light sources, can affect how effectively the key source is diminished."

CHRISTOPHER GREY is a professional photographer whose career spans over thirty years and almost every photographic discipline. His current work includes portrait photography, stock photography, and national and regional advertising photography for The Midwest Dairy Association (Got Milk?) and other clients. He also writes a monthly column on professional lighting techniques for ShootSmarter.com and teaches lighting at ShootSmarter University in Aurora, IL. For more on his lighting techniques, be sure to read *Master Lighting Guide for Portrait Photographers* (Amherst Media, 2004). Samples of his work can be seen at www.christophergrey.com.

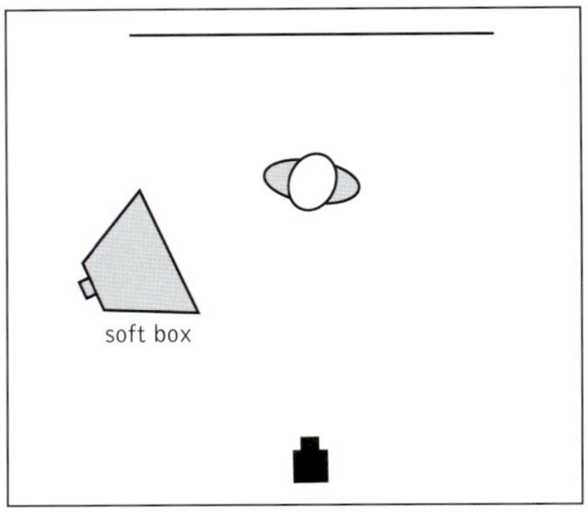

FAR LEFT AND ABOVE—A medium soft box was placed about six feet from the subject. **LEFT**—Here, the same soft box was placed about one foot from the subject.

FAR LEFT AND LEFT—Here, that same soft box is about as close as you can get—roughly four inches from his cheek.

"Tied directly to the Inverse Square Law is a little sub-truth we call 'depth of light,'" continues Grey. "In simple terms, this means that for every position of the source, whether it's near or close to the subject, exposure is constant for a certain portion of the distance across the subject. In *really* simple terms, the farther the source is from the subject, the more even the exposure, front to back, across the subject. Conversely, the closer you move the source to the subject the faster the light will fall off; your 'depth of light' will become more shallow the closer you get."

"The key for the simple one-light scenario seen in this series of images was a medium soft box," says Grey. "For the first shot (top left), the subject was placed six feet from the background to pick up some spill and keep him from dropping into shadow. I placed the key light six feet from him and metered off his camera-left cheek, letting the shadows come. The shadow detail is a result of light bouncing around the studio; there were no fill cards in use."

To create the second image (top center), Grey moved the key light to about one foot from the subject's cheek. "Notice how the depth of light decreased, but the shadows remained about the same," he says.

The bottom two images on this page show how close you can get—about four inches away—and still keep enough background for this composition. The depth of light is extremely shallow, but the highlights are clean and the shadows deep and full of detail. "Look at the setup shot (bottom right)," says Grey. "I wasn't kidding when I said the light was close!"

TOP RIGHT—Grey set his background light, a six-inch dish, about six inches from the paper. **FAR RIGHT AND DIAGRAM**—With his model in position, Grey moved in an 18-inch dish and 40-degree grid to light the subject's face, setting the key about two feet from the subject. **BOTTOM RIGHT**—The 18-inch dish was then changed to a six-inch dish with barndoors.

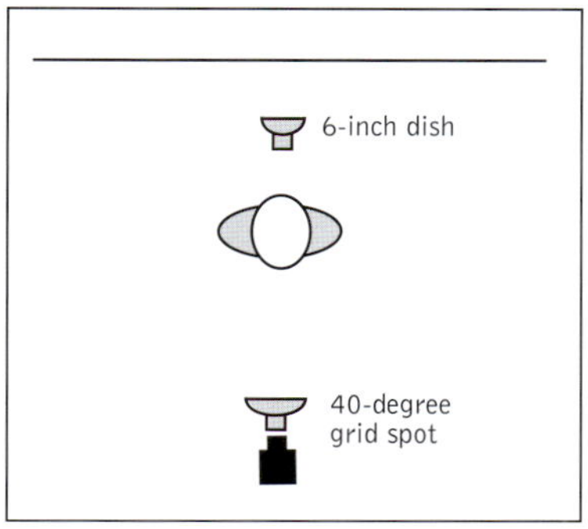

For the next falloff portrait (top right), Grey first set his background light, a six-inch dish on the strobe placed about six inches from the paper. "Inside the specular circle, the exposure was too hot to read, but it read f/22 at the edge of the diffused highlight, so that determined the power output that was needed from the key," says Grey. With his model in position, he moved in an 18-inch dish and 40-degree grid spot to light his face, setting the key about two feet from the subject. "This is actually quite nice," says Grey, "but I wanted to boost the contrast even more and play light off the planes of his face."

The 18-inch dish was changed to a six-inch dish with barndoors, which he closed until they were only about one inch apart. "Something interesting happened when I closed the barndoors," notes Grey. "The inside of the dish was faceted to distribute light evenly, and because the opening was so narrow, the barndoors acted like a small aperture (lots of depth of field), and projected their own shape in several places (bottom right). This was unexpected, but it added something extra."

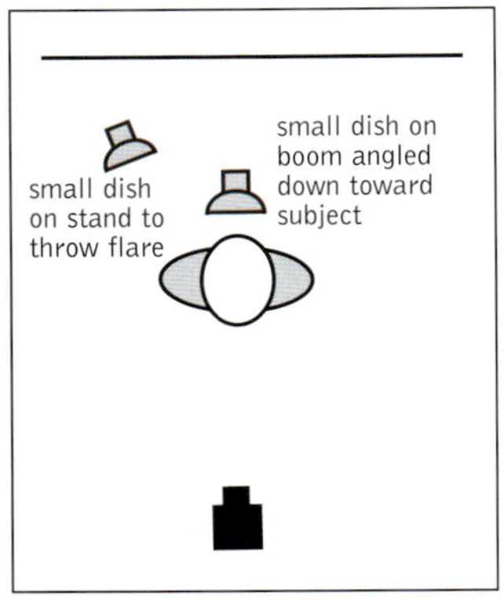

Two lights were used to create this flared backlight look. Both utilized a small dish and were balanced to the same power output, approximately four stops over the key light.

PORTRAITS WITH FLARE

If you've ever aimed your camera into the sun, you've seen what lens flare will do. While the results can be detrimental when unexpected, when lens flare is intentionally exploited, the results can be stunning. "This is an extremely variable effect," says Grey, "so I suggest you use these basic ideas until you find combinations you and your clients like." Out-of-the-ordinary techniques like this are easily tacked on to

the end of a more traditional shoot just by saying, "I wonder what would happen if . . ."

Two lights were used to create the flared backlight look seen in the first image (facing page, top left and diagram). Both lights utilized a small dish and were balanced to the same power output, approximately four stops over the key light.

When the output of the backlight is more closely matched to the key, the flaring light is still bright enough to overexpose itself but not too much of the surrounding area (facing page, bottom left).

Using a large soft box instead of a point light source reduces the lens element reflections while providing a softer flare (facing page, bottom right). The strobe head was centered just below the subject's chin and tilted up slightly toward the camera.

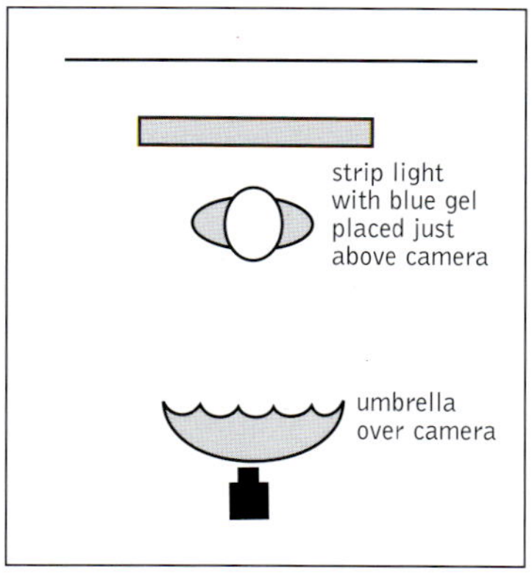

Here, a strip light with a blue filter was positioned as a hair light behind the subject but was set low enough to shine directly into the camera's lens.

For the dramatic image shown above, a strip light with a blue gel was positioned as a hair light behind the subject but was set low enough to shine directly into the camera's lens. "This effectively lowered the overall contrast without showing extra reflections," says Grey.

ONE-LIGHT GLAMOUR

"For a glamorous change of pace, source your one-light portrait from behind your subject," says Grey.

Unmodified light spreads out rapidly. For the image on the left, a single strobe with a six-inch reflector was placed far enough behind the model to light her hair evenly and cast a shadow that completely covered the camera (any light falling on the lens would cause flare). A fan added life to her hair.

Bookend flats were set in a V shape between the subject and camera then moved in or out until the lighting ratio was 4:1. "There are minor drawbacks to using the two reflectors equal angles to camera," Grey points out. "Notice the double shadows that define the inside of each nasolabial fold. While there is nothing wrong with this, it can make the face look heavier. Also, from this position, the shadow that falls across her neck completely encircles it. This could have been avoided by turning her body to face either of the two reflectors. If you look closely at her eyes, you'll also see that the tall reflectors give her irises a 'cat's eye' appearance."

To increase the contouring, Grey backed off one of the reflectors to produce less fill. For the example seen below (right), he moved the camera-left reflector until the ratio was 1:4.

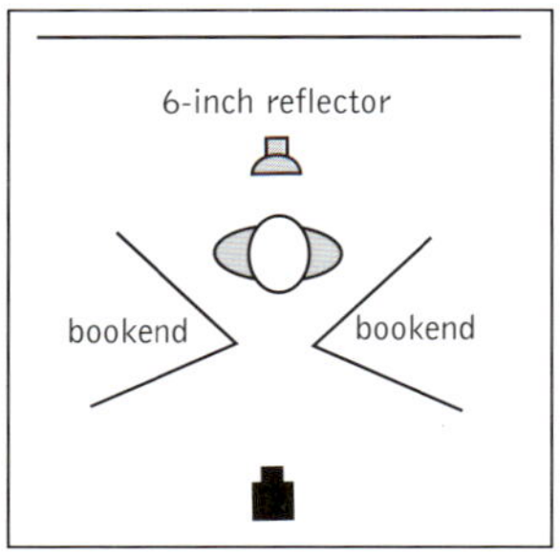

Using two reflectors at equal angles to camera, double shadows define the inside of each nasolabial fold. This can make the face look heavier.

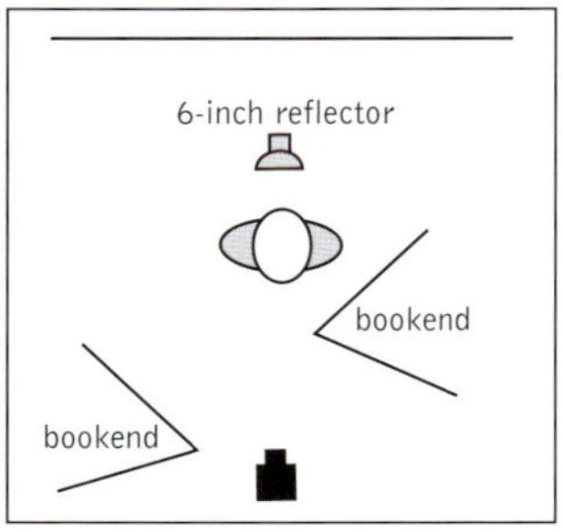

Backing off one of the reflectors reduces the fill and produces more contouring on the subject's face.

Here, the subject was almost surrounded by reflectors and soft boxes, which were set to the same exposure.

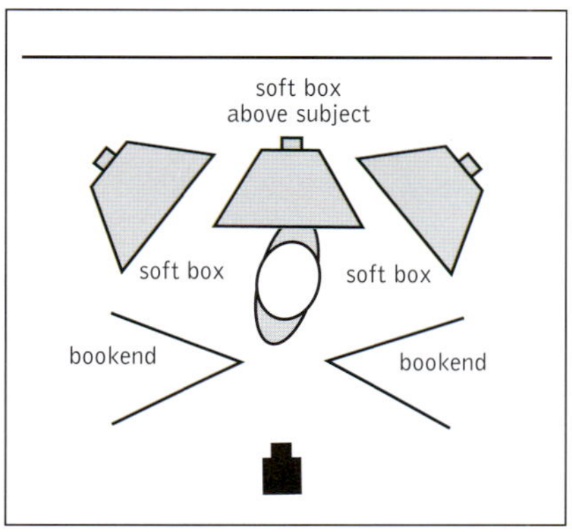

This short-light shot was lit from the left, with stray light from the source bounced into a white bookend at camera right.

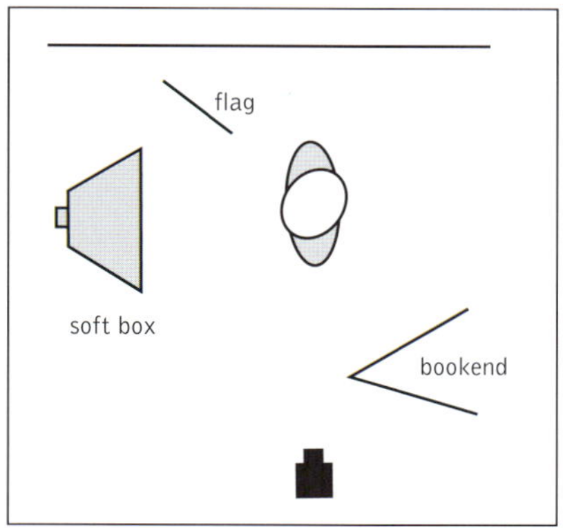

THE BEAUTY OF OVEREXPOSURE

Creative overexposure is often used to indicate a light or airy mood. For the image on the left, the model was almost surrounded by reflectors and soft boxes. She sat within inches of the background paper, which helped bounce the light around. "The light on her is actually rather flat," says Grey. "To increase the contrast a bit, the color slide film was push-processed two stops (instead of just opening the lens two stops when the image was made)."

The image on the right shows a simple setup, requiring only one large soft box and a bookend and a flag. This short-light scenario is lit from the left, with stray light from the source bounced into a white bookend at camera right. "The reflector became the key light and was moved in or out until the difference between the source and the reflection was three stops," says Grey. "A black flag was placed at an angle behind the source to throw shadow on the background and reverse the light-to-dark play on her."

HOLLYWOOD-STYLE GLAMOUR LIGHTING

"Being able to call up a technique that your client may not even have thought about can produce a positive difference in your bottom line," says Grey. The Hollywood portrait look of the late 1930s to mid-1940s is one such style.

To emulate this classic lighting, your accessory list will include grid spots, barndoors, snoots, cutters, and flags. These will be used only with direct lights, just as traditional hot lights were used in the past. Although they might be bounced off a fill card or bookend, they won't be modified by umbrellas or soft boxes. "This is the key to success," says Grey.

For the image below, the key light was tightly barndoored to almost exclusively light the subject's face. Since the key was set high to get the deep shadows of her eyes, and because it was placed close to her, the light fell off rapidly. The first of the two backlights was aimed more at her shoulder than her hair and produced the hot spot on her shoulder. It was set ½ stop over the key light. The second was aimed at her hip and was set at 1½ stops over the key light, because it was aimed at black cloth. Grey also set a small fill card just above the camera to catch some of the backlight and open the shadows.

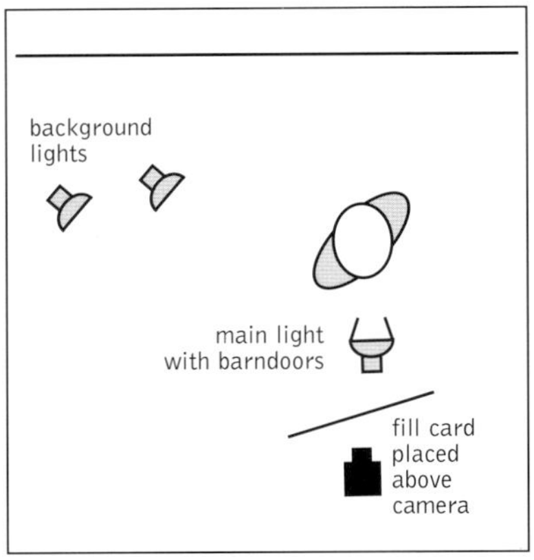

Direct lighting is one of the critical elements when creating classic Hollywood portraits.

For the images above, an 18-inch dish, with the strobe set at its lowest power output, was the key. At about five feet from the model, it metered at f/8. Grey placed a hair light on each side. The camera-left hair light was fitted with vertical barndoors, throwing light down her side. The other hair light was a six-inch dish with a 30-degree grid spot.

The background was comprised of medium-gray seamless paper and a red flat, which appears dark gray when rendered in black & white. To light this, Grey placed a six-inch dish with a 20-degree grid spot on the floor almost directly behind the model. This was aimed at what Grey calls a "reverse cookie" (shards of broken mirror mounted haphazardly on a piece of plywood) to reflect a pattern onto both surfaces.

With his model in place, Grey tweaked the lights slightly and brought the camera-left hair light closer to camera and lowered it to widen the highlight and light the side of her nose. "Originally, I had placed the key just to the right of camera," says Grey, "but I decided to move it over the camera instead. This little move gave me broad light (top left) to butterfly (bottom left). When she turned to profile, the slight move of the camera-left side light produced a perfect closed loop highlight (above)."

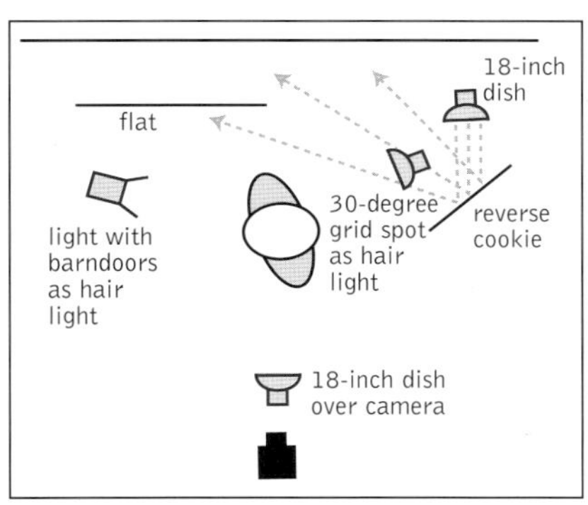

Making small adjustments to this lighting setup and the position of the model allowed Grey to create the range of looks seen above.

WORKING WITH CANDLES

"I borrowed this beautiful gown from a talented seamstress, Laura Hughes (the Bodice Goddess), who sells her wares at Minnesota's autumnal Renaissance Festival," says Grey. "My intention was to create a photo reminiscent of French Renaissance paintings, engineering in some of the flavor of the early pieces while using a contemporary subject."

Grey began by roughing in the light on Madge, his faithful lighting assistant (below). "After setting Madge to the height of my model, I set a large soft box to camera right," says Grey. "This particular box is older, and the white nylon has yellowed with age. I hoped it would give a feeling of antiquity."

Once the candelabra was in place, Grey added two sidelights. The first, set low at camera left, held a five-degree grid spot and was aimed at the part of the backdrop that would show behind the candles. A second light, with a 10-degree grid, was set higher and just to the side of the candles. Both lights were covered with Roscolux 3408, a half-tungsten acetate. The light that was aimed at her face was additionally gelled with a sheet of Roscolux 111 diffusion material to softly spread the "candle glow" without any shadows.

A small vertical flag was set to keep any of the cheek light from spilling onto the candles—a dead giveaway that chicanery was afoot (top left).

The key was set at f/11, the cheek light at f/5.6, and the background at f/5.6.5. The background light was a little brighter because the matte paint on the cloth background soaked up some extra light.

After downloading a test of Madge, Grey felt the candle glow was neither warm nor subtle enough. The gels were changed to full tungsten, which lowered the light output by an additional ½ stop and warmed the color even more, effectively solving both of these problems. A white bookend was moved in at camera left to open and soften the shadows.

"I knew from experience that I would need to face two other issues before taking the first image," says Grey. "I had determined by tests that the candles would need a one-second exposure at

TOP—A test shoot with his trusty model allowed Grey to set his lighting while the real model was having her hair and makeup done. **BOTTOM LEFT AND RIGHT**—This test revealed that, for optimum results, he would need to make separate exposures of the model and the candles.

TOP LEFT AND RIGHT—Grey added an incandescent spotlight, directed at the model's face, to narrow her pupils and show her beautiful blue eyes. **BOTTOM**—The final image is beautifully lit and captures the warm glow Grey wanted.

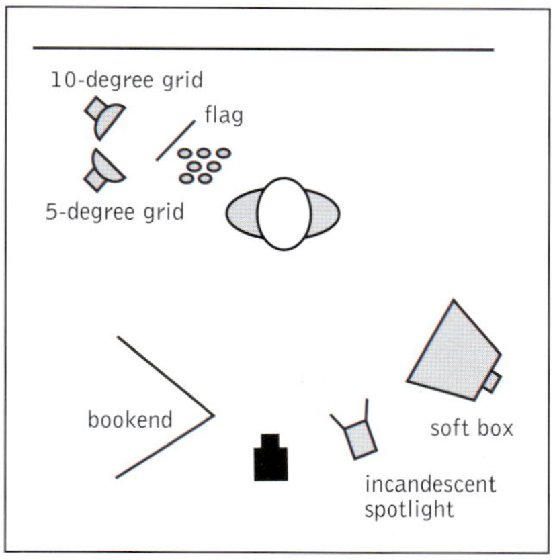

f/11 in order to register at the brightness level I liked. If I were to shoot both the candles and the subject at the same time this would mean shooting in the dark, with only the strobes firing and without the benefit of modeling lights. This would not be difficult, since the poses involved no movement. However, if I chose to drag the shutter for the full second after the strobe fired (in the dark), my model's eyes would show dime-sized pupils and no iris color. The solution was to shoot the lit candles separately, from the camera angle that I intended to use, then copy them into place later using Photoshop."

Since he no longer had to worry about the candles, he was able to spark up an incandescent spotlight, which he aimed at his model's face to narrow her pupils and show her beautiful blue eyes (top left).

After adding the lit candles and doing some additional Photoshop work, the finished product is evocative, warm, and absolutely lovely (right).

As this example shows, every time you take a picture, you practice, you play, and you learn. "The higher your aspirations as a photographer, the deeper the legacy you'll leave behind—measured one image at a time," says Grey.

11. TIM SCHOOLER

Shaping with Shadows

Most high-school seniors will never have a chance to be professional models, but when a senior arrives at Tim Schooler's Lafayette studio, in the heart of Louisiana's Cajun country, they get a taste of what it would be like. "We treat them like models for a day," says Schooler. "We don't

RIGHT—Schooler created this image on location at a farm owned by his subject's family. It was shot late in the day under a three-foot overhang, yielding soft, directional light. Schooler then rendered the image in sepia to produce a vintage look. This portrait was actually created while Schooler and his subject were waiting for the sun to set so he could get some images of her outdoors with her horse. One of these images appears on page 108. **FACING PAGE**—Schooler picked up this clay pipe with a metallic finish from a Mexican import shop because he thought it would make a great prop. To create this image, he used a 4x6-foot Larson soft box as the main light to camera left. A background light was also placed to skim across the fabric, creating the great texture you see in this portrait. The final component of the lighting was the addition of two accent lights on either side of the subject. These created the bright highlights on her blond hair.

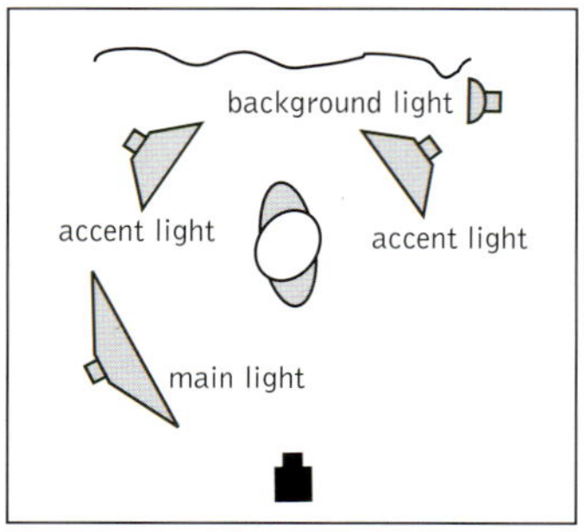

TIM SCHOOLER is a professional portrait photographer who specializes in high-school senior portrait photography. His successful studio offers a blend of traditional posing and lighting but with more of a fashion edge, producing images that appeal to both teens and parents. While Schooler is especially well known for his location lighting techniques, he is also a master of studio lighting. To see more of his acclaimed images, visit www.timschooler.com.

LEFT (TOP AND BOTTOM)—Portraits with an urban look are popular with Schooler's senior clients. In this case the young woman's outfit inspired Schooler to select an offbeat location for her portraits—an abandoned building that had its face blown off by Hurricane Rita in 2005. The destruction revealed a great shooting area, covered with colorful graffiti. To camera right the building was totally open to the street, so the opening created a soft directional main-light source. Schooler just added a little reflected fill to complete the image.

limit them in clothing changes and we take them to exciting locations that lend themselves to the fashion style of my work." The success of this strategy is evident in the sheer length of Schooler's waiting list for senior portrait sessions; it often has as many as *three hundred* names on it.

When Schooler first entered the market as a professional photographer, he operated his business out of his home. As a result, he had to quickly become a master of location lighting. Eventually, however, he saw the need to open a small studio to do cap-and-gown and other more traditional images. For many

BELOW—This young man plays seven instruments and is a big fan of old jazz music. He wanted a vintage look in some of his photos, so Schooler created this portrait of him, designing it to create the look of a musician waiting for a bus. He shot the image in the late afternoon and simply turned the subject's face toward the setting sun. He used a reflector on the shadow side of the subject for a little fill light. To finish the image and complete the vintage look, Schooler used Photoshop to create a combination sepia and handcolored look.

ABOVE—Schooler created this headshot against a rubber wall that is textured to look like bricks. "It looks so real, everyone who sees it has to touch it to believe it's rubber," he says. The main light was a 4x6-foot Larson soft box placed to camera right and quite low (because the subject was sitting on the floor). Adding a fan to the setup kicked her hair around and gave the image more of a fashion edge. **FACING PAGE**—As in the portrait above, Schooler used a 4x6-foot soft box at floor level for the main-light source in this portrait. Here, however, he also added accent lights (4x3 -foot soft boxes) to the left and right behind the subject (see diagram). These lit the brim of her hat. Because the backdrop did not match her outfit, he created the image to be used in black & white.

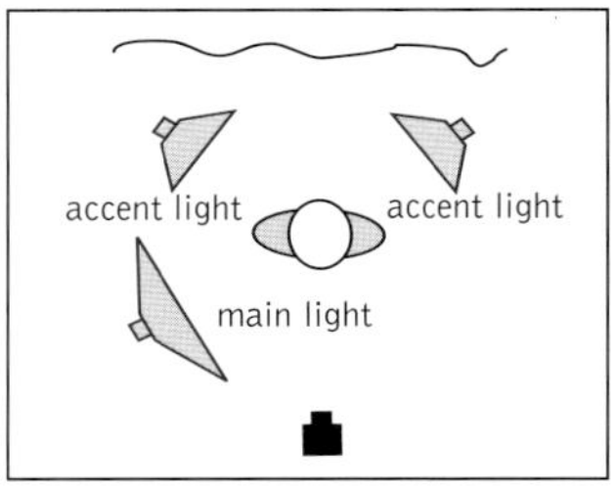

photographers, gaining the convenience and control of working in a studio would have spelled the end to much of their location photography—it's an impulse Schooler can appreciate. "Location work is difficult," he says. "It's often hot during senior season, and working in a studio is much easier."

Still, Schooler chooses to spend about half of his time on shoots outside the studio and considers location work to be part of his signature style. "My specialization in location photography has helped me create a niche market," he says. "While it started as a necessity, it turned into an opportunity when I realized how much seniors love shooting on location."

Because his time is now split between the studio and other locations, Schooler chose to locate his studio space in a downtown area. This gives him ample

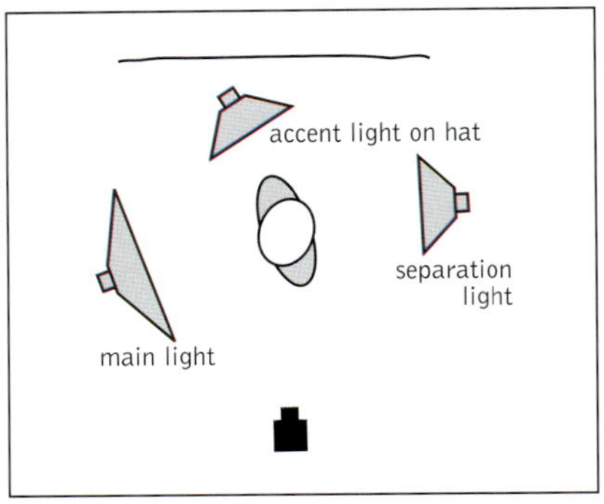

TOP—Schooler selected this Dave Maheu painted backdrop to complement the subject's outfit. He used a 4x6-foot soft box as the main light, placed low to get light under the brim of her hat. A 4x3-foot soft box accented her hat from above. An identical light was used behind the subject for separation. **BOTTOM**—To create this "fantasy" portrait, the senior was wrapped in blue fabric that was pulled out behind her and agitated by a fan. Schooler used a 4x6-foot soft box as the main light, then added two accent lights, one at waist height and one behind the subject. He used the Smudge tool in Photoshop to blend the "dress" into the background.

shooting areas all around him—and many seniors love his urban-style portraits with grafitti or brick walls in the background. For example, the portrait at the bottom of the facing page was actually created in a parking ramp across the street from his studio.

For students who want a more pastoral look, the University of Louisiana is nearby and has beautiful grounds. For some sessions, Schooler will also travel to a location selected by the student.

When it comes to lighting, whether in the studio or on location, Schooler says he is a big fan of directional light and the shadows it creates. As you can see in the portraits in this chapter, he generally avoids flat lighting effects and often produces images with a higher ratio than is favored by some photographers. The result is a dramatic look that suits his teen clients and their fashion-oriented sensibilities.

RIGHT—"As soon as they see it, everyone wants a shot like this," says Schooler. To create it, he spread white fabric on the floor of his high-key set. A 4x5-foot soft box served as the main light and was placed on the floor under the ladder from which Schooler shot the image. A 4x3-foot soft box was also placed low to skim across her hair. **BELOW**—This young man, a Christian graffiti artist, took Schooler to a parking ramp across the street from the studio to show him some of his work. There, Schooler saw this beam of light. The young artist liked it, so they created this portrait on the spot using just the available light.

Most of Schooler's portraits are also short lit, meaning that the main light source (whether it's the sun or a softbox) hits the side of the subject's face that is turned away from the camera. This produces a slimming effect that flatters most faces and also adds to the dramatic quality of his lighting—especially since it is somewhat less common than broad lighting in most portrait photography.

The other quality Schooler looks for is softness. While the shadows in his portrait may lean toward the dramatic, the transition between highlight and shadow is usually very gentle. As a result, the lighting he achieves shows great contouring but is also very forgiving and flattering.

In the studio, he achieves this look by using a large main light, typically a 4x6-foot Larson softbox. Outdoors, he also looks for large, directional sources. As you can see in many of the images in this chapter, he likes to shoot near the end of the day when the setting sun naturally provides directional light, even in open areas (see the image to the left, for example).

TOP—For this senior portrait, the subject wanted an image with her horse, Joe. Schooler and his subjects just waited until the sun was setting and created the shot in the last twenty minutes of the day's light. Waiting for this moment was critical because the field was completely open, so no overhead obstructions were available to soften the light or give it some direction. **BOTTOM**—Schooler says that many of his senior portrait clients bring their prom dresses to their sessions. When the skirt of the dress is very full, a shot like this shows off the dress better than a shot with the young lady standing. Here, Schooler shot down from a ladder. The main light was a 4x6-foot soft box, and a hair light was used over the subject. An accent light was also employed behind the subject to camera right. This image was created on another Dave Maheu background. **FACING PAGE**—With about twenty minutes of light left in the day, Schooler posed this senior on a bed of fallen camellia petals. He shot from above the subject to fill the background with the red petals. With late-day sun hitting the subject from behind, Schooler simply feathered light from a reflector onto her face to complete the late-day glow.

For these shots, Schooler worked with the sun very low behind his subject. The backlighting added a glowing edge light that highlighted her hair and helps separate the subject from the background. Posing her under a tree added some direction to the light. All Schooler needed to add to the naturally existing lighting setup was a little reflected fill light to open up the shadows.

Schooler is also a big fan of Dean Collins and his subtractive lighting techniques. Since he does so much of his lighting on location, Schooler often uses this technique to produce directional lighting effects where none exists. This may be as simple as finding an area where the subject is naturally blocked from above by a tree (as in the photos shown on this page), a porch, or some other overhang.

Schooler also carries a collapsible black reflector to his location shoots. If he needs to block the overhead light and create some direction, he uses this as a gobo and has an assistant hold it in place while he shoots. This is a great way to "add" light to one side of the face by actually subtracting it from the other side.

With such setups, Schooler adds a reflector that is feathered toward the the subject's face in the direction the main light is coming from. This gently fills the shadows and adds a little "pop" to the eyes for a vibrant look.

Ultimately, what Schooler is looking for is a three-dimensional look in an inherently two-dimensional medium. Like Rembrandt, one of the great pioneers of realistically rendering human faces, Schooler knows that the key to creating the look he wants is the use of shadow. Seeking soft light with a directional quality, he achieves this goal quite beautifully.

12. GEORGE SIMIAN

Seeing Something Extraordinary

George Simian is a successful commercial photographer who lives and works in Los Angeles (although his assignments take him to many other locales, as well).

Born in Romania, his interest in photography took root at an early age. Says Simian, "My father was an amateur photographer and I was fascinated with it—especially as a ten- or eleven-year-old when I watched him photograph my schoolmates' singing and dancing performances." He adds with a laugh, "I also discovered that you could actually possess pictures of the most attractive girl in class!"

Simian was a teenager when he and his parents moved to the U.S. It wasn't until he met a graphic design professor at Cornell University, however, that he began his move from hobbyist to professional. "Even though I was going to a huge school," he recalls, "there was no photography offered, but this professor offered it as part of his graphic design course. I took the class and then offered to be his teaching assistant. He took me up on it and I started teaching a photography section within his course. I loved it and stayed on to teach photography for a couple more years."

Simian was soon asked by Polaroid Corporation to do some PR photography. "Ironically," he says,

For this shoot at a park, Simian took out a sheet for the kids to sit on—but the little girl started running around with it as a cape. Based on this idea, Simian had the young man hold the sheet up behind him and adobt a "tough guy" look. Not to be outdone, the little girl jumped back into the frame with her own tough look. Moments like these are why Simian favors natural-looking light for images of kids—children are dramatic enough without any special effects! Here he used just the ambient light with fill from a large reflector.

GEORGE SIMIAN is a commercial photographer, but his images are more portraits than general "people pictures." Because he strives to make each shoot a personal encounter that captures a unique moment in time, his photographs are inbued with a warmth and spontaneity that many commercial images lack. Simian attended Cornell University, where he both studied and later taught photography. He has recently relocated from New York to Los Angeles, where he is busy establishing his photography business and teaching photography at Julia Dean Photography Workshops and UCLA Extension. To see more of his work, please visit www.GeorgeSimian.com.

FACING PAGE (TOP)—For this image, created as part of an advertising campaign for Capital One (a large bank), Simian paired strobe on the subject with continuous light on the background. To render the background blue, he used an HMI light and a very cool filter on the camera. Existing fluorescent fixtures overhead added some green tones. The subject was posed under a black fabric tent to protect her from spill. A warm gel on the main light neutralized her skin tones. **FACING PAGE (BOTTOM)**—The same basic setup was used for this image except that it was shot in a hallway with windows that added a warm color to the background. This was accentuated by the use of a warm filter on the lens, producing a sunset look. The strobe main light was, again, filtered to neutralize the rendition of the subject's skin tones. **RIGHT**—This image of a software company executive had to be edgy. Simian shot the portrait in a staircase, using ambient light from the glass wall behind her. A blue filter on the lens rendered the dramatic tones in the background. Again, he placed a black tent over the subject so she was illuminated only by the main light, a medium Chimera. Notice the extreme blur in this shot. It overruns some of the subject but it's appropriate to the intent of the image. For all of these images, a large white sheet placed opposite the main light provided soft, open fill.

"the job interfered with my teaching schedule and I had to get a substitute for a couple of classes. I soon got called by the department chair and was asked to choose between being a 'photographer,' implying an art photographer, and a 'hack.' So I did a little math in my head. I was getting paid $200 a day to be a PR photographer versus $200 a week to teach—that was in 1977. I reluctantly agreed that I was going to be a hack. That was the beginning of my commercial career."

Through Polaroid, Simian met a graphic designer who took him under his wing, first as an assistant and then as a second shooter. That relationship continued for over a dozen years and Simian ended up doing the photography for many of the designer's annual reports. "That spread my reputation and led

ABOVE—This image was created during a shoot for Johnson & Johnson. While the planned image showed the kids washing the car, Simian also created some variations. For the shoot, he borrowed the car and the dog from a friend, then drafted some kids from the small town in Connecticut where he was working. The car was parked in the shade, and two large Chimera soft boxes were placed about three feet from it (you can see them in the reflections on the car). The trees in the background were actually green when the image was shot. To make it look like an autumn day, Simian used two warming gels over the lens. This amplified the effect of the sunlight (which was already warmer than the strobe on the kids). Adding a little camera shake made it look like the leaves were blowing in the wind. Of course, adding all that warmth on the lens meant Simian also had to use a complementary filter to cool light from the strobes to keep the skin tones realistic. With all this filtration, he needed 4800 watts of power just to shoot at f/4! Because the main light was relatively frontal and there was lots of ambient light, he didn't need to add a fill source. **FACING PAGE**—George shot a number of images as this little girl climbed and jumped around wildly on a rock wall. When she suddenly became calm, he snapped this tranquil portrait. The light on the subject was from two medium Chimeras. The light on the background, which was quite close to the subject, was from the Chimeras and some ambient tungsten. While he could have blurred this more using camera shake, that wouldn't have been appropriate to the suddenly still subject and the tranquility he wanted to show. Instead, he relied on a shallow depth of field to separate the subject from the background.

to other annual report clients," he says, "which led to a career in shooting annual reports."

DEVELOPING A LIGHTING STYLE

Just as Simian's career has evolved, so too has his approach to lighting. Looking back on his amateur days, he describes himself as a "handheld, black & white, street-photography kind of guy." In those days, he was always looking for soft light, so many of his images were taken with window light or open shade.

When he got his first auxiliary flash unit in the mid-1970s, he discovered he could bounce light off the ceiling or (with the flash not mounted on the

FACING PAGE—The subject of this image is a car mechanic who happens to be a violinist in his spare time. To create the shot, Simian took the subject to a church that had been converted into condominiums. He posed him in a stairway that featured the huge stained-glass window that forms the background of the image. There was daylight coming through the window, so George used a blue filter over his lens to cool the background. He then lit the subject with a large Chimera soft box placed low and close to the subject. "This isn't a normal placement," notes Simian, "but this subject could take it." The soft box was gelled to compensate for the blue filter on the lens. After the shoot, Simian used Photoshop to enhance the saturation and contrast of the image. **ABOVE**—This image was created for a paper company brochure and features a famous graphic designer. On the screens surrounding him are examples of some of his work, although Simian chose to render them subtly and almost abstractly. The main light for the image, a small Chimera fitted with a warming gel, was placed behind the monitor seen in the foreground of the image. To light the background and ceiling, Simian used HMI light sources with blue gels. The effect was enhanced by the use of a blue filter on the lens. The shadows on the subject's face are darker than in most of Simian's portraits. The reason? The setup was so tight that there was no room to add a fill source.

FACING PAGE—Simian used one of his students as a model for this image taken at a coffee shop. The main light was a Chimera in front of the subject and to camera right. The background was lit by window light on the right and existing tungsten light on the background. A light used to illuminate the coffee machine also added a little hair light on the subject. Simian usually avoids hair lights, as he feels the results don't look natural. Here, however, it's effective. The image was finished in Photoshop by reducing the brightness of the windows in the background. **RIGHT**—After a commercial shoot at this location, Simian obtained permission to return the next day with his own model to create an image for self promotion. He used a large Chimera soft box from camera left as the main light. A cool gel was placed on this to compensate for a warm filter used on the lens to make the background glow. A black fabric tent over the subject kept her skin tones just a little warmer than neutral.

camera) off a nearby wall. It was a big improvement over direct light, and the bounce technique was something he continued to employ when he made the transition to lighting with strobes.

The next evolution in his lighting strategy was the development of what he laughingly calls "George's Wall of Light." This consisted of an 8x8-foot shower curtain suspended between two light stands. This was used to transform his small strobe sources into one huge, diffused main light. It provided great results—especially for a photographer on a budget!

When he finally purchased his first Chimera soft box he was delighted with the results. Soon, he discovered the wonderful results he could achieve when lighting the subject and the background separately and differently. Using this strategy, he could keep the viewer's focus on the subject while still allowing the background to set the scene. His basic strategy was to place the Chimera very close to the subject for a soft but directional source of light. He would then light the background separately and with a different look; the light might be a different color, harder, or have a different direction, for instance.

At the same time, Simian was spending a lot of time in rock clubs. There, he worked with small cameras and on-camera flash. To avoid the cave-like backgrounds this produced in the dark clubs, he started manually dragging the shutter. This brought in the ambient light, but because he needed to handhold the camera, the images that resulted often had jiggly backgrounds as a result of the continuous light combined with handheld camera movement.

Eventually, this look migrated into his commercial work, where the jiggly background helped soften distracting elements and keep the viewer's attention on the subject. But there were a few issues.

"I wasted a lot of money buying strobes that didn't have short enough flash durations," recalls

LEFT—This image is the essence of simplicity. Simian created it in a barn using the soft and directional light from an opening to camera right. He boosted the ISO setting to 1600 to work with just the available light, then finished the image in Photoshop by removing a slight color cast on the left from some weak fluorescent lighting in the barn. **FACING PAGE**—Simian shot down from a ladder to use a wood floor as the background of this image, which was created for the Bon-Ton department stores. The floor was lit with a tungsten light placed right down on it. The main light on the subject was a Chimera, placed somewhat lower than normal. While Simian usually employs reflected fill, for this image he used a tungsten source placed behind him. This image called for some camera movement to create the dark halo around the subject. Because he used a continuous source for the fill light, however, he also produced squiggly catchlights and a soft blur in the shadow areas that were illuminated by the fill source. Note, however, that the highlight areas are still tack sharp.

Simian. The $^1/_{250}$-second duration on these units was fine for the limited camera movement incurred when handholding, but when he wanted to create more dramatic blurring by jerking the camera, he ended up with unacceptable blurring or ghosting on the subject. As a result, he switched to the Swedish-made Profoto line, which offers flash durations on the order of $^1/_{1500}$ second. While these cost four or five times as much as their slower counterparts, they are also very sturdy and reliable—a big asset for Simian, since all of his work is done on location. They also have good safety features and a large frosted-glass dome over the tube, which Simian appreciates.

The other problem with this technique is that the blur effect can overrun the subject in unappealing ways. To combat this, Simian has refined his technique to isolate this run-over in the shadow areas of the subject. Because the critical highlight areas of the portrait are sharp, though, people rarely notice the slight blur in the shadows.

A CHALLENGE WITH DIGITAL

Some clients, of course, want the background to be at least reasonably sharp. In these cases, Simian uses strobe on the foreground *and* the background, relying on depth of field to create the separation he wants. While this was simple with film, with digital it's become more of a challenge. As a result he often finds he needs to shoot with a 3-stop neutral density filter over the lens in order use his lenses' widest apertures. While this resolves the depth of field issue, it makes it harder to focus and dramatically dims the ground-glass screen. It also means he needs lots of power in his light sources.

WHAT HE LOOKS FOR TODAY

Today, Simian essentially looks for ways to make the most of each situation. "I want to create lighting that is appropriate to the client, the message we are trying to communicate in the photo, and the design—whether it's trendy, classic, dramatic, etc." This can be a real challenge, since all his images are created on location and he often has just a few minutes after arriving to decide what he's going to do.

Still, there are a few basic qualities he tends to look for in a lighting setup. One quality he favors is soft lighting from the side. "I'm still enamored with

This image was actually created in a room with solid white walls. Using a cookie to cast shadows on the walls, then blurring those shadows with camera movement, produces a much more interesting background.

window lighting," he says. He also looks for a soft gradation of light across the face and, more often than not, turns his subject's face into the light.

When it comes to the background, the light needs to make sense. Often, he chooses a direction that is opposite to that on the subject—but if there are windows in the scene, the light on the background must appear to come from them or it will be distracting (see the images on pages 118–19 for examples).

THE EFFECT OF COLOR

One of the things you'll instantly notice in Simian's images is that he's not afraid of color. "I'm interested in the psychological effects of color," he says, "and how it can be used to communicate mood." As a result, the people in Simian's images are typically neutral to warm—and often they are *very* warm. They are never, however, a strange or unappealing color. These warm tones are both appropriate to human skin tones and offer another way of making the subjects jump out from the backgrounds, which are more often rendered in cooler tones.

To accomplish this, Simian carries a variety of colored gels to each shoot, as well as a number of light sources (tungsten for orange or yellow backgrounds; HMIs for blue, green, or cyan backgrounds). He may also use on-camera filtration with a complementary gel on the main light to keep the subject neutral while adding color to the rest of the image (although he does this less with digital than he did with film; digital's custom white-balance settings have greatly simplified his workflow).

However, because he's often employing a shutter-drag technique to blur the background, he must be careful not to allow the colored light on the background to spill onto the subject. To prevent this, he often uses a black fabric tent over the subject.

ONE LOCATION, MANY LOOKS

On many assignments, Simian needs to create a variety of looks in one location. On a recent job, he had to photograph nearly fifty individual subjects in one boardroom and make each portrait look different.

To accomplish this, he uses cookies, blockers placed between the light source and the background to cast interesting shadows. When he first started using this technique he simply employed objects he found on location—plants, wire hangers, grills from fluorescent lights, etc. Then, he switched to panels made from foam-core board with openings cut into them.

These were hard to transport, however, so now he uses thin sheets of black plastic into which he has had his wife cut different shapes and arrangements of holes—round holes, square holes, big holes, small holes, etc. These 3x4-foot sheets roll up easily but are rigid enough to hold their shape. He carries about a dozen such sheets to most shoots.

Once the shapes are projected onto the background, the addition of camera movement renders them as an overall texture rather than a series of circles or squares. Using this technique, Simian can quickly transform a boring white wall into something much more interesting (see facing page).

CONCLUSION

"My images are portraits," Simian says. "Some of them are quiet, some of them are more spontaneous, but they're all an encounter. They're all my looking at someone and getting excited and saying, 'Look at them—aren't they wonderful? Aren't they interesting?' It's really about making this connection and seeing something extraordinary in this person and in this moment."

In this way, Simian's current work still bears a close relationship to his father's photographs—the images that first intrigued him back in Romania. "I was inspired to start in photography by the model of my father, who was basically creating a family album," he says. "Now, even though I'm photographing other people's kids, or corporate executives, I still have a sense that these images are meaningful both personally and as historical documents of what someone felt at a particular moment in time. I love creating them, because they are valuable both to me and to the subject."

After photographing this executive in a professional setting, Simian got together with him and his kids for an informal portrait. When he walked into the television room, he saw a stack of remote controls, so he had everyone grab one. He also turned the television to form the foreground of the image (in this shot, you can see a baseball game in progress). Behind the television, Simian placed a Chimera softbox. The other light comes from the tungsten sources he added in the room. Using a long exposure, Simian created a portrait that combines sharp and blurred areas to great effect, capturing the energy and fun of this family.

CONCLUSION

When it comes to photographing people, the tools that today's photographers have at their fingertips are almost limitless. How these tools are applied, on the other hand, varies widely. Some photographers favor complex, highly technical setups that offer the ultimate in control; others rely primarily on available light to produce images with a more natural and spontaneous look. Some photographers strive to get everything in-camera; others take advantage of digital postproduction to finesse their images and transform one or more "raw" images into a final shot that reflects their creative vision.

Yet, despite these differences, all the photographers profiled in this book agree on one thing: you have to be a master of light to succeed as a professional photographer. As you've seen, despite the countless changes in photography with the advent of digital capture, lighting techniques (especially those based on a solid understanding of the physics of light) remain one of the most portable skill sets you can invest your time in acquiring. Regardless of the capture method, the way light behaves remains the same.

If there's one other constant in photography, it's that successful photographers never stop learning. The artists featured in this book have a great deal to teach others about lighting, but they all remain students of lighting as well. Each photographer I spoke with mentioned seminars they had attended, books they had read, or other photographers whose lighting techniques they admired. Not only is this continuing education critical to keeping up with the ever-changing demands of the marketplace, it's also important for continuing to evolve creatively. If you stop learning and trying new techniques, it can be hard to maintain your enthusiasm—and it will show in your images.

Thanks again to all of the photographers who graciously contributed their time and images. And to readers: study their advice and experiment with the techniques that work for them; they are an excellent starting point and source of inspiration. Ultimately, however, they are all tools—tools that are best used in helping you to refine and achieve your unique creative vision. Good luck!

INDEX

OTHER BOOKS FROM

Amherst Media®

ALSO BY MICHELLE PERKINS

BEGINNER'S GUIDE TO ADOBE® PHOTOSHOP®
3rd Ed.

Learn to effectively make your images look their best, create original artwork, or add unique effects to any image. Topics are presented in short, easy-to-digest sections that will boost confidence and ensure outstanding images. $29.95 list, 8½x11, 128p, 300 color images, order no. 1823.

COLOR CORRECTION AND ENHANCEMENT WITH ADOBE® PHOTOSHOP®

Master precision the color correction and artistic color enhancement techniques needed to perfect your scanned images and digital photos. $29.95 list, 8½x11, 128p, 300 color images, index, order no. 1776.

THE PRACTICAL GUIDE TO DIGITAL IMAGING

This book takes the mystery (and intimidation!) out of digital imaging. Short, simple lessons make it easy to master all the terms and techniques. Even if you're an absolute beginner, you'll get on the fast track to better imaging. $29.95 list, 8½x11, 128p, 150 color images, index, order no. 1799.

DIGITAL LANDSCAPE PHOTOGRAPHY STEP BY STEP

Using a digital camera makes it fun to learn landscape photography. Short, easy lessons ensure rapid learning and success! $17.95 list, 9x9, 112p, 120 color images, index, order no. 1800.

DIGITAL CAMERA TRICKS AND SPECIAL EFFECTS 101

With a digital camera and basic image-editing software, creating eye-popping special effects is amazingly easy! Using simple materials and techniques, these step-by-step lessons get you started quickly. $14.95 list, 6x9, 96p, 120 color images, index, order no. 1906.

OUTDOOR AND LOCATION PORTRAIT PHOTOGRAPHY, 2nd Ed.

Jeff Smith

Learn to work with natural light, select locations, and make clients look their best. Packed with step-by-step discussions and illustrations to help you shoot like a pro! $29.95 list, 8½x11, 128p, 80 color photos, index, order no. 1632.

CORRECTIVE LIGHTING, POSING & RETOUCHING FOR DIGITAL PORTRAIT PHOTOGRAPHERS, 2nd Ed.

Jeff Smith

Learn to make every client look his or her best by using lighting and posing to conceal real or imagined flaws—from baldness, to acne, to figure flaws. $34.95 list, 8½x11, 120p, 150 color photos, order no. 1711.

PORTRAIT PHOTOGRAPHER'S HANDBOOK, 2nd Ed.

Bill Hurter

Bill Hurter has compiled a step-by-step guide to portraiture that easily leads the reader through all phases of portrait photography. This book will be an asset to experienced photographers and beginners alike. $29.95 list, 8½x11, 128p, 175 color photos, order no. 1708.

THE ART AND TECHNIQUES OF BUSINESS PORTRAIT PHOTOGRAPHY

Andre Amyot

Learn the business and creative skills photographers need to compete successfully in this challenging field. $29.95 list, 8½x11, 128p, 100 color photos, index, order no. 1762.

PORTRAIT PHOTOGRAPHY THE ART OF SEEING LIGHT

Don Blair with Peter Skinner

Learn to harness the best light both in studio and on location, and get the secrets behind the magical portraiture captured by this award-winning, seasoned pro. $29.95 list, 8½x11, 128p, 100 color photos, index, order no. 1783.

BEGINNER'S GUIDE TO PHOTOGRAPHIC LIGHTING

Don Marr

Create high-impact photographs of any subject with Marr's simple techniques. From edgy and dynamic to subdued and natural, this book will show you how to get the myriad effects you're after. $29.95 list, 8½x11, 128p, 150 color photos, index, order no. 1785.

LIGHTING TECHNIQUES FOR

FASHION AND GLAMOUR PHOTOGRAPHY

Stephen A. Dantzig, PsyD.

In fashion and glamour photography, light is the key to producing images with impact. With these techniques, you'll be primed for success! $29.95 list, 8½x11, 128p, over 200 color images, index, order no. 1795.

MASTER LIGHTING GUIDE

FOR PORTRAIT PHOTOGRAPHERS

Christopher Grey

Efficiently light executive and model portraits, high and low key images, and more. Master traditional lighting styles and use creative modifications that will maximize your results. $29.95 list, 8½x11, 128p, 300 color photos, index, order no. 1778.

DIGITAL PHOTOGRAPHY BOOT CAMP

Kevin Kubota

Kevin Kubota's popular workshop is now a book! A down-and-dirty, step-by-step course in building a professional photography workflow and creating digital images that sell! $34.95 list, 8½x11, 128p, 250 color images, index, order no. 1809.

THE BEST OF PHOTOGRAPHIC LIGHTING

Bill Hurter

Top professionals reveal the secrets behind their successful strategies for studio, location, and outdoor lighting. Packed with tips for portraits, still lifes, and more. $34.95 list, 8½x11, 128p, 150 color photos, index, order no. 1808.

MARKETING & SELLING TECHNIQUES

FOR DIGITAL PORTRAIT PHOTOGRAPHERS

Kathleen Hawkins

Great portraits aren't enough to ensure the success of your business! Learn how to attract clients and boost your sales. $34.95 list, 8½x11, 128p, 150 color photos, index, order no. 1804.

THE BEST OF FAMILY PORTRAIT PHOTOGRAPHY

Bill Hurter

Acclaimed photographers reveal the secrets behind their most successful family portraits. Packed with award-winning images and helpful techniques. $34.95 list, 8½x11, 128p, 150 color photos, index, order no. 1812.

PROFESSIONAL MARKETING & SELLING TECHNIQUES

FOR DIGITAL WEDDING PHOTOGRAPHERS, SECOND EDITION

Kathleen Hawkins

Taking great photos isn't enough to ensure success! Become a master marketer and salesperson with these easy techniques. $34.95 list, 8½x11, 128p, 150 color photos, index, order no. 1815.

ARTISTIC TECHNIQUES WITH ADOBE® PHOTOSHOP® AND COREL® PAINTER®

Deborah Lynn Ferro

Flex your creative skills and learn how to transform photographs into fine-art masterpieces. Step-by-step techniques make it easy! $34.95 list, 8½x11, 128p, 200 color images, index, order no. 1806.

MORE PHOTO BOOKS ARE AVAILABLE

Amherst Media®

PO BOX 586

BUFFALO, NY 14226 USA

INDIVIDUALS: If possible, purchase books from an Amherst Media retailer. Contact us for the dealer nearest you, or visit our web site and use our dealer locater. To order direct, visit our web site, or send a check/money order with a note listing the books you want and your shipping address. All major credit cards are also accepted. For domestic and international shipping rates, please visit our web site or contact us at the numbers listed below. New York state residents add 8% sales tax.

DEALERS, DISTRIBUTORS & COLLEGES: Write, call, or fax to place orders. For price information, contact Amherst Media or an Amherst Media sales representative. Net 30 days.

(800)622-3278 or (716)874-4450

FAX: (716)874-4508

All prices, publication dates, and specifications are subject to change without notice. Prices are in U.S. dollars. Payment in U.S. funds only.

WWW.AMHERSTMEDIA.COM

FOR A COMPLETE CATALOG OF BOOKS AND ADDITIONAL INFORMATION